Men. Women. Relationships.

Men. Women. Relationships.

Surviving the Plague of Modern Masculinity

Paul Elam

LPS publishing

This collection of essays contains the truth as I see it. It's not pretty and it's not comfortable but it's honest and I've taken care to make sure I've expressed it with my trademark lack of candy coating. Please proceed with caution. — PE

LPS publishing
Kemp House
152 City Road
London
EC1V 2NX

lpspublishing.wordpress.com

Table of Contents

Foreword

In 2018 President Donald Trump said, "It's a very scary time for young men in America." His statement resonated around the world, being the first head of state to openly point to this "elephant in the room" truth about modern men. He was, of course, referring to false allegations made by women which, even when proven false, are treated with impunity.

Inherent in Trump's remark is an acknowledgment that false accusations are designed to inflict maximum damage, eliciting a veritable torture chamber of punishments, whether it be social ostracization, banning from social media, various kinds of deplatforming, fines, loss of home, job, children, assets and so on - or worse, incarceration or death by mob violence. It is no wonder that it is a scary time for men.

The net result of this and other forms of misandry is the production of obedient, servile males; automatons in service of a society dominated by women and their concerns. The pattern is hardly new, being recognized a century ago by George A. Birmingham who in 1914 observed, "American social life seems to me - the word is one to apologize for - *gynocentric*. It is arranged with a view to the convenience and delight of women. Men come in where and how they can."

Despite this state of gender relations the majority of men, including red pill men, are either in relationships or want to be, but are lacking strategy on how to navigate them without losing their lives. They don't want to come in 'where and how they can,' like two-bit stage extras in a low rent play, however they may not have an alternative strategy mapped out. How then, might men navigate intimate relationships with such a stacked deck?

Enter Paul Elam, who provides a powerful analysis of these issues based on years of experience in working with men. In the following pages he analyzes various strategies on offer both within and outside the manosphere, highlighting their pros and cons before tabling a red pill strategy of his own based on the cultivation of strong personal values.

Elam emphasizes that, biologically speaking, men are pair-bonders who are more likely to seek long-term relationships despite obvious dangers. With this in mind he suggests that it makes sense to develop strategies for successfully navigating relationships in place of remaining ideologically rudderless and thus vulnerable to harm. He asks how we might satisfy our need for human attachment and community without becoming a casualty of the same, while taking time to offer practical suggestions.

The essays in this book reject the repackaging of traditional gynocentrism, romantic love, chivalry, empty salves of pussy hounding, feminist-framed sycophancy, or alternatively the nihilistic retreat from both relationships and the world that may end up doing more harm than good – strategies that frequently contribute to the emptiness a man was hoping to escape at the outset. On these and other topics Elam acts as an iconoclast moving to smash false idols and their supporting ideologies while offering an alternative way forward based on personal liberty and the values that support it.

Anyone reading this book will recognize immediately that it is the work of a master hand, distilling a formidable amount of knowledge into a series of essays that will assist men in developing their own map of meaning. With the long-awaited publishing of this collection of essays, men who seek a better way to navigate the world will get nothing short of a red pill bible.

Peter Wright

Gynocentrism and its cultural origins (gynocentrism.com)
Gynocentrism: From Feudalism to the Modern Disney Princess (2014)

Books edited by Peter Wright:
A Brief History of The Men's Rights Movement: From 1856 to the Present (2017)
Feminism and The Creation of a Female Aristocracy (2018)
Books co-written with Paul Elam:
Red Pill Psychology: Psychology for Men in a Gynocentric World (2017)
Chivalry: A Gynocentric Tradition (2019)

Acknowledgements

Now I know what people mean when they say they could not have written a book without the help of others. I've many people to thank for this one; for their help, their inspiration and for their important influence on my work.

To Erin Pizzey for demonstrating to the world what courage against ideological hate looks like. To Warren Farrell, for The Myth of Male Power. To Peter Wright, who educated me in ways that only he could, and for the unshakable, unfailing support. To Alison Tieman, whose work had probably the greatest influence on my thinking. To Janice Fiamengo, for "getting" what I do and why I do it; for not taking the easier path. To Karen Straughan, for being brilliant and not taking the bait. To Mike Buchanan for all his tireless work in the face of overwhelming odds, and for the years of supporting AVFM. To Tom Golden, for the support, friendship and the encouragement to be who I am and nothing else. To my friends in Australia. And to you, Harry, wherever you are.

Finally, to my partner, Stacey, who stood by me all these years as I did my best to walk what I talk, and for the countless hours of work dedicated to supporting my efforts to be a voice for men.

Introduction

First, some words about Perseus and The Medusa on the cover of this book. I'm sure it could be a bit of a head scratcher; a book on relationships presented with the image of a man holding up the head of a woman that he has just severed from her body. I can almost hear the screeching of feminist harpies as I write this into the book's introduction. O.K., so that much is good.

Still, there will be people other than feminists; rational, thinking people, who may take issue with the imagery. I respectfully remind them that Perseus was a god and The Medusa was a monster. Mythical characters, both of them. Neither are accurately representative of men or women respectively. The intent of drawing from the story of Perseus and Medusa the Gorgon is to punctuate the idea that solving relationship problems requires the slaying of some demons. In each other and in ourselves. It does not mean, for the hopelessly literal among us, that we cut each other's heads off.

The point of all this comes into focus when we consider the deteriorating state of modern relationships, especially given our collective inability to discuss those relationships honestly. This is particularly relevant where men are concerned. What men want and expect from relationships most often turns out to be vastly different from what they end up getting. I know this because I've spent most of my adult life watching men pursue relationships into a brick wall; witnessing the damage that happens when fantasy collides with reality. The only way for men to make that train wreck worse is to talk about it honestly, openly and without apology.

So, what the hell, let's do it anyway.

This book is dedicated to an examination of how men enter relationships wanting and expecting love, companionship and regular sex in a trusting partnership. It's also dedicated to how men end up running themselves to exhaustion on a loveless, sexless hamster wheel, trying to satisfy women who are constitutionally incapable of being satisfied. More importantly, it is dedicated to jumping off that hamster wheel; to rejecting the yes-man their relationship demands and becoming the man they were intended to be.

That will either improve the relationship drastically or end it. Either way will deliver relief in the long run. Getting there is necessarily a rough road. For men who have been damaged by embracing unhealthy fantasies about women, the corrective experience requires them to abandon those fantasies. They must see women, not as they want them to be, not as they hope for them to be, but as they are. The Sugar and Spice narrative must die. Like men, women are flawed, imperfect specimens of humanity. Unfortunately, our culture fails to advise women of that in the same ways it advises men of their flaws. Society, being an equal opportunity enforcer of fantasy, coerces men to remain silent about this.

In fact, what society does is prohibit any objective evaluation of women. It's praise or nothing, and it better be praise. If you point out that women are emotional, and they most certainly are, you're accused of hating women. If you point out that women feel entitled to be treated better than men, which a great many of them do, you face the same allegation. If you point out that women tend to complicate relationships and sabotage problem-solving with immaturity and irrationality, well, then, you get the picture. Don't you, you bad, bad man?

So, this raises the question. If we can't talk, even in the most abstract terms, about the problems most men face with women, how on earth do we expect men to contend with those problems in day to day life? Because, news flash, those problems are there whether anyone wants us to talk about them or not.

Instead of teaching men to speak honestly about these issues, we've taken a different path. For about the past thousand years, we've expected men to bury themselves in false mythology about women and about themselves. We've distorted honest self-perception with imagery of valiant knights; stoic men of strength who face and destroy dragons to protect damsels; hardly the kind of men who are affected by mistreatment in a relationship. Men just 'man up' and deal. Complaining, about anything, is not in their supposedly manly nature.

This would work brilliantly if only men knew their place and complied. And to some extent, they do comply. You can see the results in suicide statistics, rates of alcoholism, drug abuse, depression and disease. That isn't an excuse. It's just a fact. One of many we are better off dealing with honestly.

The cost of chosen ignorance about all this is men who are more prone to escape into the refuge of a bar or into drugs, or affairs or violence. Or they just bury themselves in work, in anything that keeps them out of the home as much as possible.

Some men, a growing number of them, voice their concerns about women by making the choice to avoid them altogether. MGTOW, or Men Going Their Own Way, is a growing phenomenon. It's men of all ages swearing off marriage, and in many cases swearing off cohabitation with women. In some cases, it's men swearing off all contact with them.

Their motto is simple. Don't get married. Don't take the risk or suffer the frustrations that comes with modern women. They've written women off and, at least to their thinking, have solved the problem. After all, you don't have to deal with the pitfalls of modern women if you don't commit to one to begin with. Think of these men what you will, their way is healthier than engaging a life that ensures abuse and the inability to talk about it.

Still, as many MGTOW as there are, most men can't or won't go in that direction. They want to fulfill their biological programming, and their personal desires, by pair-bonding with women. And that, Dear Reader, only brings us back full circle to the original problem.

The pair-bonding men want and earnestly hope for isn't often the pair-bonding they'll get. Without a new narrative about women and a new mythology about relationships, the only place they'll have to go is back on the familiar path of failure; back on that hamster wheel. No matter what men think, no matter how different any woman they meet may seem, the result will always be the same. You can't create a new story without changing the underlying mythology.

That is what this book is about; teaching men to view themselves, women and relationships differently than they ever have before. It is a difficult, rocky path that requires something different than men have ever expected of themselves. It requires them to accept that there is much more to life than a woman's acceptance, and that a woman's approval at any cost is a price too high. Sometimes a woman's approval is the last thing you need. Those sentiments and more blaze across all the pages you are about to read. They can change your life for the better if you want. And if you don't, that's O.K., too. There's always room on the hamster wheel.

Men

Servant, Slave, and Scapegoat

> *"The modern hero, the modern individual who dares to heed the call and seek the mansion of that presence with whom it is our whole destiny to be atoned, cannot, indeed must not, wait for his community to cast off its slough of pride, fear, rationalized avarice, and sanctified misunderstanding. 'Live,' Nietzsche says, 'as though the day were here.' It is not society that is to guide and save the creative hero, but precisely the reverse. And so, every one of us shares the supreme ordeal - carries the cross of the Redeemer - not in the bright moments of his tribe's great victories, but in the silences of his personal despair." Joseph Campbell ~ The Hero with a Thousand Faces*

Anyone claiming to help men, psychologically speaking, has an obligation to place their philosophy front and center for men to see. I also understand that most practitioners don't really do that, especially in what I loosely define as the "mental health" industry.

Usually, what you get is a short and sputtering list of platitudes about "wholeness," finding your "inner this" or "inner that," accompanied by an obscure definition of the practitioner's approach. It's either that or you just get the bill.

Sometimes, often actually, they will inform you that they subscribe to feminist theory, which is an admission of their complicity in undermining men and enough reason to view them with disdain.

This book is intended to demonstrate exactly what men need and are not getting, specifically in their more modern struggle for identity and an understanding of where they fit in the world. This is particularly important as the lack of those things may well result in some serious problems. Among them are family dysfunction, substance abuse, suicide, violence, anxiety, depression, shame and a lack of self-respect that often crosses the line into self-hatred.

It is not that the current crisis of male identity is the sole cause of these problems. It certainly isn't. For example, family dysfunction is a self-perpetuating malady passed down from parents to children. In and of itself it has little to do with modern masculinity. Alcoholism is not a "male problem," nor is violence or other forms of abuse. Those are not gendered issues regardless of what those practicing under a feminist shingle try to tell you.

When assessing problems, it can be very difficult to tell the difference between cause and symptom, between a problem and its source. Does family dysfunction cause substance abuse or is substance abuse the cause of the dysfunction? Is violence at the root of relationship problems or do relationship problems fuel and promote violence? Do communication problems cause hostility or does hostility cause communication problems?

Are all these problems symbiotic, just a teeter-totter interaction of various pathologies feeding each other? If so, can we ameliorate one problem by successfully intervening on another? I don't think we'll ever know for sure.

We know with certainty, though, that solutions begin with a recognition that there is a crisis in male identity and male self-respect. It affects all of us, gay or straight, black or white and other races, regardless of religion or socioeconomic status.

Fifty years of gender politics have thrust men into a world of sexual relations with the rules stacked against them. We are now three generations of men who have been pummeled with messages of who we are, almost all of them wrong. And we've been incessantly informed of who we are supposed to be, almost always to our detriment. We are not the rapists-in-waiting that feminist have painted us to be. We are not the abusers. We are not the oppressors. We are not emotionally deficient or morally impaired. All of these are hateful lies furthered by gender ideologues.

Our mental health industry is one of the prime proponents of these misguided ideas. Those ideas are espoused, for profit, at the expense of men and boys, largely because they sell to women. We badly need a revised view of men; a new path for them. And that starts with a look back into our collective histories.

The Old School Archetypes

The classic, historical masculine archetypes are Hero, Villain, Ruler, Warrior, Creator, Sage, Rebel, and Explorer, all of which define what men were driven to be. They also provided a model of what men did not want to be. They gifted men with a sense of identity and purpose, a rudder for their navigation of life. To a great degree (with some downsides) they worked. Jungian analysts, in the days before the ideological corruption of psychology, would likely tell you that these archetypes are rooted in our biology.

It is also important to note that all these archetypes are anthropomorphic projections of the human male experience. They took root in our earliest mythologies because they were already in play in human life. Strangely, "mythology" told the real story of our lives. Every epic battle, great journey, tragedy, and triumph of mythical figures mirrored the internal and external experience of real human beings.

And so it went from epoch to epoch.

All that has been supplanted with a new and toxic narrative. We now live in a zeitgeist where all male archetypes have been reduced to that of Villain, with the expectation that they will assume the role of Hero when needed...and directed. The ongoing expectations of men to protect, provide, sacrifice and endure have not changed. The change in narrative, however, demands that recognition and honoring of those things cease in favor of persistent demonization.

Similar changes have happened in the lives of women. The Manipulator, the Bitch, the Saboteur, the Queen and the Damsel in Distress have usurped the timeless archetypes of Mother (Demeter), Daughter (Persephone), Lover (Aphrodite), civic life and learning (Athena), etc. While all these and other female archetypes are on full social display, the spectrum of those archetypes has begun to degrade into a vacillation between two roles based on immediate perception.

Women are now universally seen as the Queen unless they are in distress or claim to be in distress. Once the perception of female distress registers, social consciousness reverts them to being the original Damsel in Distress. It is as though they live in a perpetual state of flux between empowered and helpless, depending on which is more advantageous, just as we see play out today across the landscape of sexual politics. That, too, is ultimately heading for a crisis of identity in women, though for the purposes of this book, we need not explore that further.

The denial of all this and the assumption that it has not had a tremendous impact on the psyches of men has left them in an emotional and social wasteland.

This leads to an inescapable conclusion. While men do need assistance with specific problems, they are also suffering in a famine of functional archetypes. Seeking to help men without recognizing the deficit in archetypes is like putting a band-aid on a tumor.

If we are to help men, it requires us to enable them to nurture a new narrative of themselves and their lives. They need new archetypes that foster a new sense of identity if they are going to thrive in a new age.

So, what exactly is an archetype?

The Greek root words are *archein*, meaning "original or old," and *typos*, meaning "model or type." Archetype: Original model. Archetypes are the old, original models on which men unconsciously shape and mold their lives.

Perhaps in the days when there were payoffs, e.g. honor, appreciation, respect and status, men's unconscious movement toward one archetype or another made more sense.

We do not live in those times anymore, and we haven't for most or all of your lifetime. What remains for most men in modern life is a world of expectation without reward, burden without honor and service without self. It's the life of a servant; of a slave, and with the modern propensity to heap blame on the shoulders of men as though they were designed for that purpose, it's the life of a scapegoat.

These are the archetypes for modern man. These are the roles he's been relegated to in the view of the world he built. And it brings us to where we are, living in the age of the Great Betrayal. A world that has turned on its fathers, sons, brothers and husbands. A world that demands men sacrifice then spits in their face for their troubles.

Most men know on some level that this is true, but many have a hard time facing it. They fear a loss of social approval, a loss of "love" and a loss of what they imagine is the only space the world grants them.

Some of the fear is at least superficially warranted. Facing these issues means reaching a level of consciousness sufficient to make you a bad fit in the world of the walking blind. It means a new mythology with new archetypes born of a newer and more accurate picture of the world.

The daunting challenge is that men can no longer afford the luxury of allowing biology alone to write their story. Technology and ideology have rendered that too dangerous. The old model makes men far too easy to manipulate and far too willing to comply with the manipulation. You can find this same story throughout classic mythology, so it's nothing new. Sampson and Delilah. Odysseus and the Sirens. Those were cautionary tales informing men of the dangers of gynocentrism. These were the moral lessons of the time, which today have been erased from the cultural consciousness. The results of that resemble a modern genocide of the male soul.

Fortunately, that which has been forgotten can be learned again. And that which has been learned in error can be corrected. The fruits of that effort are precisely what men need.

Again, men tend to avoid this work out of fear. They think that change on this level will bring social and sexual death. The risk, however, of embracing this is largely an illusion. Once you walk the newer path you will likely find you don't want to return to the old one. The feigned, conditional approval of others loses its luster when the vision clears and life is brought into focus.

It's quite simple. You can start with almost any problem in life; relationship and family issues are a good start. Map the mythology that got you there, that determined your actions and reactions. Were you playing the role of the Hero? The Warrior? Were you surrendering to the Siren's Song? Was the Damsel in Distress a façade with a Witch behind the surface?

Did a faulty narrative of your place and worth in this world lead you directly into a painful wall? And if that is true, do you have the fortitude to face it and change the story?

Imagine the consciously constructed mythology that would lead you to a better place with better people. Imagine the story of you being written by your own hand, guided by your own values.

The path to get there isn't always easy, but it's made much more accessible when you make the decision to clear your own way; when you are at the helm, navigating for yourself; the stars in the sky arranged according to your own dreams and desires; when you realize and accept that there are no victims, only volunteers.

How many miserable professional men out there can remember a time when they aspired to be artisans, writers or similar creators, only to watch those dreams buckle beneath the oppressive weight of a story that they did not write? How many desperate men are clinging to the role of provider and protector, having become automatons in loveless, abusive marriages that have ground their self-respect into the dust?

How many men have stories that end with a bottle of Scotch and a handgun because they cannot breathe and do not know where to find free air? How many men would have found that free air if only they had simply chosen to pursue it?

Men need an alternative to the new mythology's archetypes of Servant, Slave and Scapegoat. The only thing preventing that from happening is the choice to cling to a narrative they did not produce and which has never served them.

We have seen the results of men living in a world that refuses to honor them or care about their struggles. How can men cope in this sort of world? How can therapists or anyone else help a man move from this restrictive, prison-like consciousness into a more truly masculine path that embraces his well-being, self-interest, and happiness?

That is what this book is about. A challenge to men to author a new narrative of their life, and a reminder that doing so is their sacred, personal responsibility. As men, whether we flourish or flounder depends entirely on whether we assume that responsibility. The politics of victimhood don't earn men the same support it has women. We are not creatures served by our own weakness.

We are, in our finest hours, Warriors, and Warriors do not suffer the weakness of men who shy from taking charge of their lives.

Pussy Begging International

You see them popping up regularly in the Manosphere; comments about the pitfalls of western women, particularly the dark and dreaded American Woman, followed by a recommendation to find a nice foreign woman.

Relationships from overseas are a growing business, and understandably so given the temperament and relative worth of so many women in North America. There are a growing number of bloggers who belabor that point, demonstrating their naivety in the process.

I'm not really coming down on them. Most of us know there is enough truth to what they are saying to make Jesus smile. But I am a little concerned with the implied idea that hypergamy isn't a danger if you put your stock and your cock in a foreign bride. She only knows how to say, "Me love you long time," with enough sincerity for a bit part in a Kubrick film. Don't be crazy (or stupid) enough to believe your ambitions for a lasting traditional family will be satisfied on a website.

Still, if you're insistent, there are countless places that can 'help' you with the hookup; places where women from Eastern Europe to the most remote of Southeast Asian shitholes catalog themselves row on row like whores behind plate glass windows in Amsterdam. All of them are making their pitch for a ticket to the Promise Mall.

These wannabe immigrants have threatened a lot of women and feminists in North America. Vaginacrats in government have been given marching orders to do something about it. The state of Maryland is leading the way on trying to strangle this business with regulation.

Make no mistake; legislation designed to make it difficult for men to look outside their own culture for a wife is a purely preemptive ploy to keep you as available fodder for western white girls. Besides, you might even decide to go ex-pat on them and take your future western dollars with you to another country. These people want your money to be stolen right here at home and redistributed to the good ol' girls club.

It's shaping up like a competition between different crime families, each angling for who is going to shake you down.

And there is an ironic twist here. concern Maryland's mail-order bride legislation was not furthered from any concern that American citizens might be duped by foreign nationals out of a cake made with their assets and iced with American citizenship. No, it was out of for those poor little wenches and what us American Male Losers might do to them once we get them over here. The mandated background checks are on *us*, not them.

Jeannie Haddaway-Riccio, Maryland's Secretary of Natural Resources, said the bill would close the loopholes in current federal law and alert would-be foreign brides, who often come from poorer countries, of the criminal history of their suitors.

Did I say ironic? Make that ironic and virulently hateful.

Of course, any legitimate needs assessment would favor a law to check out the potential bride, but as using sex and love to con men out of money isn't illegal it would probably do little good.

Education beats legislation in matters like this. The best preventative measure we can take is providing a primer on the pitfalls of international pussy begging.

This requires an armchair analysis of men who are spanning the globe in search of someone to drain their wallets and/or break their hearts. As far as I can tell, this breaks down into three kinds of men.

First, **Men Who Can't Get Laid**. Yes, even in an age where women are slinging no strings ass like it was free crack, there are men who can't manage to drum up any action. These guys exist and their solitude and loneliness lead them to desperate measures.

This first category also includes guys who can get laid but only by the fat girl who's still sitting there when the bar closes. They are stuck in Uglyville with no roads out of town. The thought of being condemned forever to life between the legs of an Andrea Dworkin lookalike makes them dangerously depressed. These guys want #1 fucky-sucky and they are going to pay to get it, often dearly so.

The next in the line of potential victims is the **Disenchanted Traditionalist**. This is the guy who wants a wife and a family but has seen enough of his own culture to know that casinos have better odds. He has too many friends in post-divorce life driving POS rust-buckets, spending every other weekend with disgruntled children who have grown to hate his guts with the ex's steady guidance.

This guy's problem is intelligence. He's smart enough to read the writing on the wall about marriage in the west, but dumb enough to think the solution will come waltzing out of *la migra*– looking like a Penthouse model and ready to cook dinner. And, oh yeah, because she comes from a "traditional culture," she won't ever divorce him and take everything the law allows.

Of course, she won't. Never, ever. Cupcake would never do that.

Eye roll.

The third and final kind of man is one for which I have some measure of sympathy. I call him the Special Needs Romantic, or **Romantard**. This guy's ambitions are simple. He just wants to be loved, and he has looked around in his own environment and found it lacking. This problem is complicated by the fact that his idea of loving a woman is akin to that of a puppy whining on the back porch to be let in. He figures that a poor woman from Guatemala will be grateful enough to leave the door open for him all the time.

She likely will until she learns about twenty words of English. Then he may find that her first complete utterance of American English is "You treat me like slave. I call lawyer now."

To some degree or another, this poor schmuck also lives in the other two kinds of men, but the true romantard is a kind of psychotic purist. He cares only for loyalty and dedication; true friendship, partnership and most of all, acceptance. He craves these things so much though, that he deludes himself into thinking he might be able to order them on the internet.

Of course, the fundamental problem here is shared by all these men. They are not trying to escape American women; they only think they are. They are trying to escape *hypergamy* - that universal sociobiological component that drives human females to constantly extract a better standard of living from the men who cross their paths. Love, devotion, traditional values *and country of origin* have nothing to do with it.

Trying to circumvent hypergamy with a mail-order bride is like trying to circumvent gravity with a trampoline. Even bouncing with all their might, these guys are not going to defy physics. But many of them get high and off course enough for a very hard landing.

The mail-order bride industry is infested with enough scams and cons to give Bernie Madoff a run for his money. The internet has a rather robust repository of the results of those ruses for anyone who wants to do the research.

There are a multitude of scams; too numerous to mention them all here. There are even scam agencies that expose other agencies' scams in order to appear more trustworthy.

You can see in their advertising they have a great awareness of our terrible trio of men. Their messaging is tailored for those men.

Sorry guys, but the jury came in on this one a long time ago. Mail-order brides are not a way around hypergamy; they are a prime example of it. These are all women who want a better standard of living than the men in their countries can give them, so they are willing to bunk up with a stranger, even someone whose language they don't speak, in order to get what they want.

Are there good, decent, traditional-minded women in Guatemala, Russia and The Philippines? Sure, there are.

Are any of them posting profiles on the internet to marry a stranger who will bring them to the U.S.?

What the hell do you think?

Honestly, how any man thinks he is going to get a traditional marriage or find love or loyalty or partnership by hiring an airmail whore is a question in need of an answer. The closest you are going to come to an answer is to look at the parallels between traditional marriage and prostitution. There are many. At least enough to make most married men edgy.

On the outside chance that what I am saying finds its way to some men contemplating this foolhardy path, let me make a couple of suggestions.

One, don't.

Two, yes, that means you.

Seriously, if you want to pay for sex, get a real hooker. They're more honest. And they ultimately cost far less than a wife, whether indigenous or from overseas. For the price of plane tickets overseas, you can have sex with a porn star.

But, on the other hand, if you can imagine the possibility that you are worth more than investing your life, your money and your heart in begging for pussy, then stay right here and keep reading. Take the Red Pill and start learning about life outside the bonds of female approval.

The self-worth you get from that will attract more women than you can imagine, none of which will be able to put you on a leash.

Why Men Can't Say No to Women:
A Historical Perspective

Men are only as mentally and emotionally healthy as their ability to say no to a woman. That bears repeating. **Men are only as mentally and emotionally healthy as their ability to say no to a woman.**

Obviously, this does not apply in some areas. Mental health problems won't be solved by simply finding a woman and uttering the word "no" in her general vicinity. Still, I will hold to this proposition and do my best to explain it. I can tell a great deal about a man, his boundaries, his values and ultimately his integrity and character with a simple measurement of his obsequiousness with and deference to women. To be frank, I never befriend or trust a man who grovels for the approval of women. It's only a matter of time before he stabs you in the back.

To understand all this requires a bit of a history lesson, dating back to the twelfth century and the cultural movement driven by Romantic Chivalry.

At precisely that moment in history, the warrior code was co-opted and harnessed to the emerging culture of courtly love, an aristocratic invention that saw the military principles of honor, gallantry and service placed at the feet of new Commanders-in-Chief – courtly women.

As historian Jennifer G. Wollock summarizes, "The idea that love is ennobling and necessary for the education of a knight comes out of the lyrics of this period but also in the romances of knighthood. Here the truest lovers are now the best knights."

While there is arguable evidence that protection of women and children is a basic male instinct tied to reproductive access, this is likely the first known time in history where that mandate was codified.

Over a period of a few hundred years, Romantic Chivalry spread to all the principal courts of Europe and found its way more broadly into the lives of everyday men and women who coveted the lifestyle of the upper class. It also fostered a great deal of female privilege and the mindless value on neoteny that came with it.

So went the first known institutionalization of pressuring men into a tradition of male servitude – or obsequiousness – toward women that continues unchecked today. Yet it was only the first of three foundational events that would become the prevailing model of gender relations; one that negatively impacts men's lives and mental health.

The next developmental watershed in men's deference to women was the Industrial Revolution. While thrusting humanity into modern civilization, it was the next giant step toward normalizing a standard of mental illness in men where it concerned their relationships with women.

Prior to the Industrial Revolution, men largely worked in or near their homes. They worked as artisans, farmers, producers of livestock, tradesman or some other profession that they passed down to their sons and other apprentices through mentoring. While still driven by the force of Romantic Chivalry, they were as involved in the raising of children as mothers were. Those mothers, by the way, also had laborious duties that were a regular part of their role in the family. With the combined work of both parents and participation of the children, families operated more like business concerns than what you most commonly see today.

Discipline and nurturing from both parents were immediately present; males and females equally influenced the lives of their children.

The Industrial Revolution, combined with Romantic Chivalry, accelerated the problems. The mass migration to cities began. Fathers were removed from the home (and the daily lives of their children) to go into factories and work. Mentoring largely died within a generation. And, of course, one of the first products of that revolution was advanced technology in the home, making the lives of women much safer and less arduous. It also created more free time for women, arguably time for them to become fixated on their emotional needs.

The impact of that on family dynamics hit like a tsunami. Women were left to the increasingly softening work of home and children alone.

They were left in want of adult company. Husbands returned from long, grueling days of labor needing food and rest without the luxury of making up time they had missed with their families.

In this familial void, women quickly turned to their children, particularly male children, to fill their emotional needs. And fathers, consumed by work and duty, largely just enforced the wishes of the mother on the children. This triggered the second wave of privilege and psychological neoteny in western women and where men, due to resentment over their absence, began to be demonized.

This greatly increased the likelihood that mothers would form inappropriate bonds with their male children in order to fill the holes in their lives. In other words, we took a step toward a society of emotional incest.

This is difficult to overstate. What I am defining here is an entire society of emotionally incestuous bonding between mothers and sons. The implications of that are tremendous, and in fact, they seem to have been verified by the following 150 years of advancing cultural malaise.

Perhaps it is not coincidental that the onset of the industrial revolution also saw the first formations of what were known to be Henpecked Husbands clubs; groups of men who gathered to use peer pressure to induce each other into tolerating more demands and abuse from their wives.

The Industrial Revolution gave birth to a new age in civilization. It also ultimately resulted in the breakdown of the family unit as it was once known. The late nineteenth century rang in the Tender Years Doctrine, and with it the first legal presumption that younger children were better off in the care of mothers than fathers. The steamroller did not stop there, it accelerated. The same glut of time and resources that spawned women to create an emotionally incestuous culture also produced gender feminism, the last and final of a monumentally powerful triad of events that left most men in seemingly inescapable servitude to women.

Barely one and a half centuries from the first American factory being built and our culture is all but dominated by a "woman-first" mentality. So rote and mindless have men become that they allow single mothers to effortlessly continue the spread of emotional incest and other forms of child abuse.

Our boys enter an education system completely dominated by female teachers, all of whom are a product of the same forces that created the new paradigm.

Society, especially the female-dominated realms of home and early education, produces males that are highly, often terminally dependent on female approval. By the time boys get more substantial exposure to adult males, the pattern is set. Not to mention the fact that the males they are exposed to are as dependent on female approval as those who might otherwise provide mentoring. They too, as beta enforcers, put pressure on boys to participate in the incestuous bond as expressed in the schools.

This puts us squarely in an age of crippled masculinity. We have legions of men who have stood by silently while their families have been destroyed in corrupt courts, where our young men are being driven out of education and into fields of combat and where men are more likely to support and enable these travesties than to object to them. Men's silence in the face of abuse is the mental health issue of our time and you can see it reflected most clearly in men's interpersonal relationships with women.

When I co-wrote *Say Goodbye to Crazy*, a book aimed at women who were dealing with the devastation wrought in their relationships by mentally unstable and abusive ex-wives, a substantial part of the focus was directed at husbands who lacked the ability to stand up to their former partners.

That problem is not contained to the second marriages of a handful of men. It is a sweeping societal problem that affects all men.

As you will see in the penultimate essay in this book, *Male Space is an Inside Job*, when I gave men in a treatment setting the task of focusing on themselves vs focusing on women, their immediate reaction was fear. That fear was proven justified when the men and women, both staff and clients of that facility, reacted to the men focusing on themselves instead of women with anger.

What was also proven was the dire need for men to overcome overwhelming programming and pressure.

With a catastrophic gender suicide gap and a plethora of other problems affecting men, at the root of it is men's programming to sacrifice their interests, well-being and their boundaries in order to take care of and please women.

They have lost the ability to say no. Indeed, they have never had it. Saying "no" to women is something we don't teach men. We teach them that "yes" is the only acceptable answer. The result? They are terrified of the loss implied by the very thought of bucking expectations. Men know that if they treat themselves like they matter, the world will prove to them that they don't.

Correcting this, reversing the trend, is easier said than done. In fact, it is damned hard work for most, and simply undoable for the many who lack the strength to face and walk through fear on such a primal level. It can, however, be accomplished, in stages, for the dedicated; for the Warriors among us.

The first stage is Simple Awareness and is by far the easiest. It is just education and can be had as easily as grasping the contents of this writing. Heck, reading this book could be all it takes for some men.

When men understand the forces that compel them to please women at any cost, they create the opportunity and motivation to imagine it can be corrected. With that, they can rewrite their future with women and with themselves.

The second stage is brutal. There is no other way to put it. It requires men to face the fear of ripping the emotionally incestuous bond; the foundational fear of all men, the fear that most resembles the fear of death. It means putting themselves in the jaws of the beast from which they must scratch and claw their way out. They must do it, most often, with people (often their families) jeering them in the process.

Make no mistake, social and emotional support for men struggling to learn self-care is exceedingly rare. One might say it is non-existent. The path to male wholeness is a lonely one, where self-reliance is the only thing you can count on.

Once men have emerged, though, they reach life determined by a newly shaped history, *sans* the Romantic Chivalry, *sans* the emotional incest and *sans* the gynocentrism. That brings with it its own challenges, as the road less traveled often does. But I've yet to meet a man who's sorry that he's done it.

I realize that the definitions of these stages are cursory and incomplete. After all, we are in uncharted waters here; miles from the kiddie pool. A place longed for in the unseen hearts of men.

The Legacy of Men on Their Knees

Please take a moment to study the image. It was posted to Twitter by an account called *History in Pictures* and was accompanied by the caption, "Man begs forgiveness in the Chicago divorce court. 1948."

Let's take a little thematic apperception test and put stories to the imagery. What do you imagine is going through this man's mind? Is he begging for forgiveness for having had an affair? Or is he just promising that he would pay more attention to his wife and be a better, more attentive husband than he had in the past?

Is his kneeling part of an act? Is he artificially contrite, feigning remorse because she has the upper hand and is about to, as the saying goes, take him to the cleaners?

Or is he his lover's fool, pleading with her not to leave him because he cannot imagine his life without her?

And what do you imagine she is thinking, standing there in her fur coat looking at him on his knees? Is she thinking, "That bastard hit me or cheated on me, or some other unforgivable sin and I am not taking him back."?

Or is she thinking, "Hell no, he's a loser. I can keep the house, half his money and continue having sex with the pool boy."

Maybe she's thinking, "Now I have him. He's begging. Maybe I will let him come crawling through the back door and he will think twice before he ever says no to me again."

And you know what? All of these scenarios are possible. Indeed, whatever you happen to think is the story hidden in this picture, it really doesn't matter. The point here is that a hundred totally credible stories in any given marriage could result in a man on his knees begging. Power is often hidden in plain view.

The other point here is that we are not dealing with a systemic boogeyman like feminism. We are talking about what men socially evolved to do with women. You are looking at the one true dominance hierarchy. You're seeing a man emulating the bottom line between men and women – if it isn't put in check by the man.

I don't say this as a segue into another anti-marriage rant. Avoiding marriage is a given in most of my work. The point here is something more than that.

It starts with the time of the photograph, 70 years ago, clearly a full generation before men-on-their-knees™ gave feminists the power to contaminate everything in their path.

In 1948, with our men finally back from World War II, we were just two years into the great baby boom. It was the heyday of the then modern family, marked by white picket fences, legal marriages of one man to one woman and family units that were largely expected to stay intact. It was a culture that spoke of divorce in whispers.

Yet I am sure that the people of 1948 would have had no problem coming up with their own stories to explain the scene in the picture. Divorce was far less common then, but when it happened it was no less likely to result in men-on-their-knees™ with women making life-altering unilateral decisions.

Hail patriarchy, right?

I brought all this up to say that while many men's issues are tied to feminist doctrine, we would do well to remember that feminism did little more than exploit weakness men were already demonstrating a very long time before feminist power was a thing.

Think of it this way. Most denizens of the Manosphere are familiar with the loaded gun metaphor. The rationale being not to marry because the state effectively puts a loaded gun in her hand which she can use with impunity any time she wants.

Look closer at the picture. This is the real loaded gun. And it has a man's suicidal finger on the trigger.

Not just as it relates to family court, but as it relates directly to most any of the negative things afflicting men's lives, as expressed in suicide, substance abuse, depression, male disposability and even male violence.

This is also the only power feminists have or ever have had. Without men-on-their-knees™, there would be no feminism.

We have evidence, through history, that the picture from 1948 doesn't just tell the story of a single man begging for a woman's mercy in a midcentury Chicago courthouse. It shines the light of reality on who men are. And in the worst possible way, it represents the natural order of things.

We started to see this image being expressed over 900 years ago at the dawn of Romantic Chivalry but there is no telling how long it was a looming part of the collective unconscious.

All of this is likely driven by the reptilian tendency in men to prioritize reproduction immediately after food and shelter. It's that cursed little lizard in our unconscious that ranks the opportunity to scatter seeds up there with breathable air, which our conscious mind continually rationalizes behind walls of denial. With rare exceptions, we will tell ourselves anything but the truth when it comes to women.

Gynocentrism, with all its lamented detriment to men, is seen expressed almost exclusively in the actions of men.

And so, what this boils down to is something really disturbing. We are unlikely to ever see full and sweeping change in how most men relate to women. Those of us who can be honest with ourselves, and who choose to act on what we know rationally, are an aberration; a glorious anomaly to which the world doesn't exactly take a shine.

So many of us have been relegated to the dark comedy section of the world stage. We watch, comment, grieve and sometimes roar in dark laughter about how average men allow themselves to be broken by average women. You can take that up with God or Darwin as you prefer, but it is what it is.

Blaming feminists or even women is a miss. This is men doing harm to themselves. They have grown accustomed to living life on the lower rung of the dominance ladder with women, even as those same women allege it's a man's world. And they look to continue doing it to themselves for the next few millennia.

Like I said, the prognosis is bad, globally speaking. Even if we could destroy feminism completely, men-on-their-knees™ would start the cycle again, giving women too much power in their lives. Poor bastards just can't help it.

As I am so fond of reporting, though, there is an answer to all of this for us lowly outliers. The internet, at least for the time being, is enabling an open critique of gynocentrism, and it is finally starting to reach the disparate minority of men capable of brushing aside the gynocentric fog and seeing themselves as worthy of something better.

It is providing men a range of options on what to do and arming them with Red Pill knowledge. Some, as in MGTOW (Men Going Their Own Way), just pull the plug. They look at the great big stinking mess and say no thanks. Other men take a less absolute approach and use what they know about the real nature of men and women to improve their reproductive odds, hopefully using that same knowledge to decrease their odds of big problems in the process.

Still others do something more minimal, like getting a strong prenup and taking care to evaluate a woman long enough to determine that she isn't a raging personality disorder.

Each way, of course, comes with different levels of risk, but they are all better options than men have ever been exposed to prior to the internet.

Gents, you are living in the first time in human history that men have near-universal access to a corrective response to the on-your-knees narrative. This, to me, is as good as it will ever get. At this point in my life, I am happily prepared to look at the world of men and just be satisfied to the point of smugness that all those bent knees and long looks down the nose are not a part of the way I live, or that I will ever live.

I sincerely hope that does not come off as callously indifferent to men who are suffering in ignorance and unteachable. I would not wish the consequences of blind gynocentrism on anyone. But the fact is that now we can point to a virtual Mount Everest of highly thoughtful commentary on what is happening between men and women. The truth, with truckloads of support, is a click away from anyone curious. I am all for letting Mr. Darwin take it from there.

And that is a good thing because the more this new narrative opens, the more we are seeing that a lot of men aggressively pursue the path of ignorance. I suspect that is also a function of gynocentrism. That gynocentrism, if viewed objectively, provides ample reasons for lower functioning men to stay in the dark about who they are. After all, who wants to look at themselves when it means a look down?

It's a shame that most of them can't see that a dose of introspection and a little bit of logic would bring them to their feet.

On Men, Women and Victims

There is a part of me that sparks a gag reflex when I think about dating advice claptrap. And while I am still not going to sink into such pablum, some responses to a meme I recently made reminded me of a theme I have seen echoed through parts of the Manosphere.

Suffice it to show you the meme I placed on Facebook and one of the early comments to it:

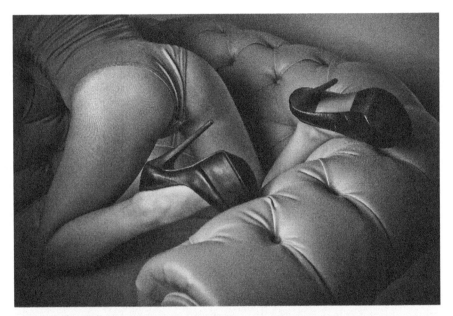

The family courts, the attorneys, the domestic violence industry and mental health professionals would like to thank you for checking out that ass without checking out her integrity and values.

And now the comment:

Too bad women have the uncanny ability to completely fake everything about them[selves] until they are married. But I like your point.

I have heard and seen this sentiment many, many times before. It is, with all respect to the man commenting, what I consider to be a copout on personal accountability.

Mind you, I get it. Women (and men) tend to enter relationships careful to always have their best foot forward. In the honeymoon phase of a new relationship, what you see is never what you really get. And that holds especially true with women. After all, it may take a long time with women before you can even see what they look like under the face paint and body enhancing clothing. Much less how they will behave when the going gets a little rough.

I know, too, that many personality disordered women have especially honed skills at "fooling" their target into thinking they are something they are not. They have refined expertise in figuring out what makes you tick and indeed an uncanny ability to project precisely what they know you want to see and hear.

They are the master of the Love Bomb and will pile on adulation and admiration from the earliest moments in the relationship, almost smothering you in unconditional approval.

So, it is easy to nod my head in agreement with the well-meaning commenter who apparently feels like he is at the mercy of women with ill-intents because he has no way of knowing better.

It is also even easier to not nod my head in agreement because I pretty much think all this is bullshit. It is a copout designed for men to absolve themselves of their responsibilities when choosing women with which they will be vulnerable. Currently, any woman you are with, in whatever circumstances, is a woman with whom you are to some measure vulnerable.

With some rare exceptions, men can screen out high-conflict, high-maintenance, high-frustration and high-danger women with a relatively small amount of consciousness and the willingness to accept responsibility for their own choices.

For some men that means taking a rather bitter dose of medicine in the form of the truth.

One, if you are sucked in by anyone in life saying all the right things at all the right times, you are what carnies call a "mark." That is the carnival crowd's term of endearment for a sucker who is just begging to part with whatever he has of value.

On the heels of that is the reality that what people *say* is generally meaningless in assessing them as a human being. Sure, some crazies out there can't talk for more than 30 seconds without revealing enough crimson flags to decorate a theme park. But for those who don't advertise their crazy so obviously (and they are legion), you need to watch what they *do*.

It's the behavior, the "what they do" part that matters. So, it's important to create an opportunity to see how they operate, what they *do*, in stressed or disappointed mode.

People almost never show you who they are with words. They do it with actions. If you are like so, so many men and you are just listening for the right words and getting all tingly when you hear them, then *you* are the one with the problem. I know, it sucks. It's unfair. As my father used to say, though, fair is what you pay on the bus.

I have long suggested that men pick a point early in a relationship to issue a firm "no" to something relatively inconsequential that she wants, and then to watch her reaction like it was the most important evaluation in their lives. That is not a stretch because it could be. Add a few more years, a few more noes and a lawyer and you have 100% assurance of being in a living hell.

If her reaction to your simple no is an immature level of disappointment; if she becomes cold and aloof, withholds sex and affection; if she responds with that ubiquitous female "fine" in a tone that promises retribution for not getting her way, then she is *showing* you everything you need to know.

One step further toward her after a demonstration like that and you have just elected to become the architect of your own misery. Telling yourself you had no way of knowing is a bit of self-delusion most men cannot afford in the long run, though there are millions of men every day who do just that – writing checks with their desire for love and sex which their bodies ultimately cannot cash.

You don't even need to create a test scenario to find out. Modifying behavior completely, even in the do-good early days of relationship infatuation, is nearly impossible. There are always tells in your line of vision.

Does she shower you with buckets of, "You're the most remarkable man I have ever met," on the third date? That is not a sign that you have stumbled onto Ms. Right. That is a sign that you are walking into a minefield and you need to quickly backtrack out of it.

Is she putting you up as some sort of savior for her physical or emotional life before she knows how you take your coffee or how you like your eggs cooked? If that is the case, and you are buying it, you might want to wake the hell up.

Healthy men don't need a pedestal to stand on. Men who are both healthy and intelligent avoid standing on pedestals like the plague. They cast a very wary eye at anyone who tries to elevate them to that level after a couple of dates.

Here's the deal, guys. Crazy women are not that skilled at hiding their crazy. Anyone who bothers to look for it can see it. In almost all cases it is only hidden from men who insist on being the monkey with both hands over his eyes. That is the real, and only, problem here.

You may point out, and quite correctly, that it is easier to suck in a man who has unresolved family of origin issues. It is indeed easier with men who have those problems. That covers a whole lot of men. They were trained to seek abuse, and they are good at it. Crazy women, the destructive, high-conflict variety, have a great deal of cold empathy and have an expansive set of tools with which to manipulate and control their mark. If the mark has unresolved family issues, it paints a bigger target on his back.

The answer is just the same as it is for anyone else. Stay out of relationships until you are conscious of how you are manipulated and controlled. Family of origin issues can be very tough and time-consuming to fully process, but it does not stop you from taking appropriate action when it is called for. As they say, "Fake it till you make it," and, "If you bring your ass, your mind will follow."

Feminism has brought us 50 years of women constructing a chasm between themselves and men. Their path is one of mistrust, distance and separatism (except from men's assets and resources). It is an ideology not of healthy bonding between men and women, but rather it is a poisoning of the ground.

Men who believe they are hapless victims of evil women, but who make no effort to screen them out based on character or values are falling right into the feminist mindset. Hostile dependency; taking any and all power you have from your enemy.

It is the worst model for male-female relations in human history. It is the relationship a young person who refuses to launch has with his parents. It's easy to get angry at anyone when the very sight of them reminds you of your own failings. Still, the hostile-dependent mindset thrives because it relies on a victim mentality, fertilized with a lack of agency and accountability. Not to put too fine a point on it, but women wear those rags a lot better than men.

Is this an endorsement for marriage to "the right woman"? No. Refusing to participate in marriage is wise because it reduces the chances that the state will wind up governing your life, and it removes the temptation for women to play that trump card, no matter how carefully you screened, should the opportunity arise.

It remains that human beings are a pair-bonding species. Marriage or not, most people choose not to fly solo. With that in mind, every human individual has a choice about who they are with. To beat a dead horse, there are no victims, only volunteers.

The more men that understand that the fewer men will end up searching pathetically for help that isn't there.

What Men Fear Most

We make heroes of men who conspicuously face and overcome fear for a good cause. However, there is one fear that we not only want men to run from; we punish them if they show any bravery at all.

There is one fear, above all others, that unites men in what we have come to regard as modern masculinity. It's a fear that affects almost all men, whether they are meek and timid by nature or the kind of men who walk into burning buildings to save people's lives.

This includes professional boxers, commercial fishermen, inner city police officers, government whistleblowers and law enforcement agents who infiltrate organized crime.

It's not a fear of death that cripples them, or of torture, or any other of the typical horrors we might imagine. Still, it's a fear so great that it has driven men to kill themselves. It has caused others to surrender their personal dignity and self-respect.

The set-up for this is almost indescribably powerful. The solution requires an understanding of how we get set up for this fatal weakness. Even the understanding requires courage to face. So much so that most men never will.

That fear is the fear of losing a woman's love and approval. It is a fear so deep and so pernicious that men will go to insane lengths to preserve the illusion of love, even when being bitch-slapped with the fact that the love isn't there and never was.

Let's look at some anecdotes that form a rather uncomfortable picture.

Why is it that so many soldiers who lay dying on the field of battle call for their mothers, or whose last words when fallen are "tell my wife I love her"? Why do so many men work so hard on salvaging relationships with women who are beyond salvage; women who have proven not only that they don't love those men but in many cases that they feel deep hatred for them?

Why do so many men never develop the skills to defend themselves from abusive women, men who volunteer to become financial marks, throwing their hard-earned cash away to impress women who could not be less interested in them? Why do men continue to volunteer labor and personal resources to women, even after they have been wiped out by them in a divorce? Speaking of divorce, why is the tendency toward suicide so overwhelmingly dominated by men during a divorce or breakup?

Why do men seem so incapable of change when it comes to how they approach getting involved with women? The decision for whether a man is going to take an emotionally, psychologically and financially invested leap with a woman hinges solely on whether she returns his physical attraction.

Nobody teaches boys how to handle these challenges. Nobody mentors them. Not fathers. Certainly not mothers. Not friends or other women. Why don't we, as a rule, ever talk to our sons about this? Why do we conspire, men and women together, to keep them in the dark and to keep them so simple-minded about women?

It's because being simple-minded (more pointedly stupid) about women is a decidedly human characteristic. It's been trained into us over the course of countless generations, all lessons hinging on the Romantic Chivalry narrative, one that demands men serve women mindlessly.

So, even though we are pummeled with the answers to these questions every day of our lives, we learn nothing. The truth slaps us in the face and screams in our ears, and we respond like we are deaf and dumb. Reality can grab us by the lapels and shake us violently, trying to get our attention, yet most men, nearly all of them, invest everything they have in not seeing, not hearing and not feeling any of it. And alas, the moment we start to pay attention at all, the fear of loss turns us away from the truth again.

I talked to a young man once who came to me for advice. He had saved up to buy his girlfriend a birthday present. It wasn't anything expensive. He was 21 and just starting out in work life. His girlfriend scoffed at the present and told him she had hoped for something a little nicer.

My advice, of course, was to get a better girlfriend or to do without till he learned to land one who was a bit less of a prostitute, but he was unable to hear any of that. He just kept circling back to his dilemma that he wanted to please her but could not afford to do so. He even asked questions about career paths, with the inference being that he did not ever want to feel so inadequate again.

When I tried to pin him down on what terrified him so **much** about her rejection, he opted to seek advice elsewhere. He exited the conversation in a bit of a huff, telling me that he wasn't, by God, "afraid of anything."

It is easy to write this off to the naivety of youth, but it is now about 15 years later and from what I hear he still lives the same way, in an endless cycle of trying and failing to make a woman happy enough to keep him around. Even though he is now married and with a child by an ostensibly different woman, he still allows her to keep him running on the performance treadmill, constantly sweating and pushing for crumbs of occasional, transient approval.

I am pretty sure he has no idea what is about to come, now that there is a child, and he has pretty much maxed out on his income potential. When the other shoe drops, and it will, he will be devastated. When and if he recovers, he will set about finding a woman much in the same way he found his wife, by overextending his means and offering it up on a silver platter to anything pretty, hoping for another crumb of approval.

How did this level of irrational, destructive fear ever become the default setting for men? Well, I think my theory on it has some weight.

The critical, formative years of every child's existence is dominated by the female presence and the female will, which is often self-serving, unhealthy and for boys, emotionally incestuous. Fathers, whether absent or present, contribute to the problem.

Where there is no male influence, the mother often runs amok. She teaches her boys that they better please her or she will punish them with rejection, physical pain and often by inflicting humiliation. For boys who have already lost one parent, this is a soul-killing, developmental nightmare and you can bet that their minds adjust with compliance.

Where the father is still present, he is often the enforcer of the same sick agenda. The term, "you just wait till your father gets home," is the young male child's first experience with proxy violence. That violence is instigated by the woman who will shape his view of all women for life, enforced by the man who will shape his view of himself and all men.

At some point, he enters the female-dominated primary education system, where his coercion into satisfying the will of women is institutionalized. By the time he reaches middle school, his preparation for how to handle his budding attraction to girls is fixed in cement.

And there is yet another key factor that puts the icing on this misandric cake: Romantic Chivalry.

For every man's entire life, he is inundated with the message of providing sacrificial, unconditional love and dedication in exchange for the appearance of approval. In fact, his willingness to place himself on the altar of female acceptance is tied directly to his ability to feel worthy as a man. As we know, an unworthy man is just about the lowest thing you can be in this culture.

The mantras of, "Happy wife, happy life," and, "When mamma ain't happy, ain't nobody happy," or their sentimental equivalents have been drilled into his consciousness from the time he was old enough to understand what "big boys don't cry" means.

Once you sweep away all the false tropes of "good man" and "a man who knows how to treat a woman," what you have left is the groveling servant produced by Romantic Chivalry.

The mindless, servile action of men with women was just a social trend that stuck around for a long time. Men weren't born fools and puppets;

it was social pressure that caused it. The human being's innate tendency for gynocentrism made it all the easier. And it continues to this day.

I recall another event from decades ago, but it will be something very familiar to you right now. I lived in a duplex. The man who lived above me was a huge sports fan, especially baseball. I could often hear the games through the thin floor of the building. One day his girlfriend was there. They were arguing because he was, according to her, watching too much baseball. I heard her clearly shout at him, "You care more about baseball than me!"

The next thing I heard was the door slamming and her footsteps going down the stairs. A few seconds later he was coming down the stairs, screaming, "Stephanie! Please wait!"

At that moment, his baseball game was still coming through the TV in his living room, unwatched. He was on the street at this point. I could see him through the window, pleading with her to stay. Just a few moments later they left together - after he went back into his flat and turned off the game.

And that is how they get you, guys. Doesn't everyone know that her threat to abandon him was her ace in the hole? Don't most or all women know this? Don't they play that card like a boss?

Stephanie's threatening to leave wasn't just a minor manipulation. She was triggering every ingrained fear he ever had from the time he was old enough to talk. Her rejection was his mother's rejection, his teacher's disapproval and somewhere in his mind there unconsciously lurked a proxy agent to punish him for his failure at Romantic Chivalry.

Of course, he wasn't consciously aware of any of this. All he knew is the thought of her abandoning him left a hole in his gut big enough to swallow him up.

She may not have been totally conscious of her actions, but you can bet she knew enough to know that in walking away she was ripping him to pieces.

When she left, she was taking his manhood with him. Just as the young woman who sneered at a less expensive present from a lovelorn young man had turned his masculinity into a cruel punchline. The only way either of these men could redeem themselves was to lose themselves. Their only path to "love" was the self-diminishment of Romantic Chivalry.

And that is the lesson; the moral if you will. Romantic Chivalry isn't love. It's just glorified begging. It makes narcissists and children of women, and hapless pawns of men, who on close inspection do not resemble anything we've ever honored about men. It robs them of true bravery. It weakens their spines. It makes them less of everything men are supposed to be.

In my way of thinking, the only way men can overcome this is by walking into the heart of their fears and rebuilding their self-image on their values. They've tried sacrificing those values to please women and it has only harmed their self-image. It makes sense that embracing their values and protecting them is the answer.

This requires rewriting the narrative of your life, starting with a vision of yourself as something other than a trained seal, balancing a beachball on its nose in hopes that the nice lady will toss it a piece of fish. I am sure you get the metaphor.

The damned thing is that doing this is harder for most men than facing a hail of bullets or running into a burning building when everyone else is running out. The fears that this kind of work taps into are more deep-seated, more profound than most men will ever even admit to themselves.

The good news is that you can start doing this anytime you make the choice. It's as simple as finding your balls and putting them to use.

How We Kill Johnny

It was three weeks after I left the last residential treatment center for which I would ever work. A Saturday morning to be precise, and the phone rang, jarring me from the rare pleasure of a sleep in. It was Camille, so I knew it wasn't good.

She wouldn't call me if it were good.

"You remember that boy Johnny you worked with, the one from Louisiana?" she asked.

"Yeah, why?"

"Dead," she said. It was uttered in the tone of someone doing a poor job acting like they didn't like delivering bad news.

"Drugs?" I asked.

"No," she replied, "Suicide. Killed that little girl he was married to, as well. And shot some guy she was sleepin' with, but he made it."

I just lay there silent.

"Anyway, I knew you would want to know."

I hung up without saying anything else. *Knew I would want to know?* My ass. Couldn't wait to tell me was more like it. Camille was an ideological crusader. She made a career of telling the men we counseled what louts they were for being men, leaving me with the part-time job, as her coworker, of cleaning up her messes. We were the only two counselors in that program and the mix was volatile. I spent many days in the administrative offices fending off complaints about my "unusual style" in dealing with male clients. "Unusual" meant that I did not view masculinity as a mental health problem.

Johnny wasn't the first tragedy in twenty years of doing that kind of work. Drug addicts sadly have a way of dying young and I have never seen evidence that the negative messages that men are pummeled with by treatment professionals are helping to change that.

I remembered Johnny's story and his pain. He was a twenty-two-year-old stock boy at an auto parts store in the hot and humid swamplands of southern Louisiana. When he spoke, it was with rural earnestness, and a Cajun accent thick as gators in bayou country.

"Man, Paul, I doan know what to do 'bout that girl o' mine. I know she cheatin'. I know I doan make a dime what she doan spend right away. Sometimes, she spend it on some other guy. But I can't help it. Every time she call my name I got to come runnin'. Lord never made a bigger fool than me."

And Johnny was right. He was a fool and couldn't be talked out of his foolishness. Just like so many "real" men. His story isn't reserved just for those who drink and drug themselves into oblivion because they have a woman they can't live with, or without.

In this awful age of misandry, we live so many lies about men that we have lost all touch with the reality of what they are really like. And the cost of it is written in caskets and countless souls lost in a world with no memory of why they died.

You see, men love. They love with the most profound intensity and selflessness of which any creature on this earth is capable. The steely bond between them and women is, unlike their hearts, unbreakable. When men die on the battlefield, they often fade away telling fellow soldiers, "Tell my wife I love her." Others cry out for their mothers as blood soaks the soil.

They are flattened by divorce, and many will eat a gun rather than face the loss, even if it is the loss of someone that has already destroyed their lives.

They will lay down in traffic for the women they love and stand in the way of bullets to protect them. And they will strike down any man who dares offend them. They have been doing this, foolishly, for the past thousand years.

79% of all suicides are men. They make up the majority of the drug addicted, the alcoholic, the depressed, the homeless, the incarcerated, the "at risk." The statistics say legions of men are suffering; that they are in danger. Yet all this has been rewritten with misandric ink. It has been revised by scholars who tell us men are bad, by psychologists whose main field of work seems to be targeting men as incomplete women, more deserving of our ridicule than our help.

The religious establishment is of little help either. In most cases, men are advised by clergy to "man up" and take full responsibility for whatever abuses they encounter in relationships. The mentality behind all this now drives our family law system, pushing men to despair and despondency with tragic frequency. That is not to even mention what it is doing to their children, whose fathers are being ripped out of their lives like bad teeth.

I hope, more than anything else, that at some point in our future, men like Johnny start to think. And that we do the same. When you see the story on the evening news about a man who set himself ablaze outside a family court, ask yourself what kind of pain could drive someone to cure it with fire? When you read in the newspaper about the man who holed up in his house with a gun and his children, threatening to take them all out, ask yourself if this is just a crazy man, or a man driven to the brink by a pain so monstrous and devastating that even the unthinkable could become an option?

The normal 4 to 1 ratio of male suicide doubles during divorce without so much as causing a hiccup in the women's numbers. Is this because men are inept at articulating feelings as compared to women? Or is it because we gleefully and with no sense of justice rip their lives to shreds during a divorce, chastising them all the while to 'man up and take it'?

Indeed, there is a great deal we should be asking. And we are. Unfortunately, all the wrong people are asking all the wrong questions. We mark Father's Days with shaming men for not being better dads, with demands for more men to "step up" and be fathers, even as we drive them from their homes like cattle.

We have psychotherapists spread the destructive illusion that women are a victim class and that men are a perpetrator class. And we have a system of higher education that is so ideologically controlling and rigid that it is nearly impossible to get honest scholarship on the problems.

All this in a culture that still raises men to put women first in all matters without even pausing to think. In fact, when men attempt to reject that form of programming the people around them can become hateful in a hurry.

That may well have been what was needed on the African Savanna three million years ago. Survival intensive environments require extreme measures. Today, however, from the comfort of our climate-controlled towers, we need to start having the difficult conversation about teaching boys more about taking care of themselves than taking care of women. That's not misogyny. It's modern survival skills and perhaps a prescription for less social violence.

Maybe if Johnny were raised not to "come running" so quickly he would have learned enough to prevent two deaths, including his own.

Perhaps the pundits, in their own erroneous way, are right. We do need better dads. We need dads to teach their sons, not "how to treat a woman," but how to hold their own with them. We don't need to teach them to "take care of their woman," but to value their own worth enough to have standards that they will hold women to other than their appearance.

And we need to teach them how rare that is in modern life. The social picture I have painted here is also an artifact of the last 50 years of radical feminism's toxic effect on sexual politics. Men and women do need to talk to each other, but in a different light than we are currently doing.

We won't have parents teaching our sons how to let bad women go if we don't have parents that are walking what they talk about the best interest of their children.

Why Men Think with Their Dicks

It seems only fitting that in this book for men that I would include a few messages for the benefit of women. After all, if you're reading this at all you've shown a remarkable measure of good character. Or, a very wide masochistic streak. Regardless of which one it is, I'd like to dedicate this to you.

First things first. Ladies, your half-baked complaints about men have a way of getting passed around like joints at an early 70's Zeppelin concert. Most of them have the same net result in the cognitive realm. Pot makes you stupid, at least temporarily. Hating on men makes you stupid and chronically angry. However, there was one of those complaints about men that resembled the truth and now I'd like to share that with the red-eyed, pissed off lot of you.

Men think with their dicks. True enough. When it comes to women, we're just wired that way. When we meet you, we size you up according to our favorite body parts first and check out the rest of the terrain as a follow-up. We wonder what you're willing to do in bed and how far you'll go before we want to know your last name.

If you're not what we want, sexually speaking, we make small talk and start thinking about an escape route, even as we nod and smile to whatever it is you're saying. If we are sexually attracted to you, everything we say and do is geared to matters horizontal. That, however, is only half the picture. Because ladies, and I want you to hear this good, you are not the least bit different. You think with your ovaries.

You look at a man's success and power in the same way he looks at your tits and ass. You wonder what he'll do with his wallet just as much as he wonders what you'll do with your mouth. Like it or not, these are the expressions of reproductive programming that are hard-wired into us as a species. It is, in the purest of forms, who and what we are. Yes, ladies, that includes you. And no, you are not the exception.

So, when it comes to men, you are better off studying them with intelligence than in playing Judge Judy. Come to think of it, taking a closer look at yourself isn't a bad idea either.

When it comes to how men and women size each other up, it's just the way things are. It doesn't make us defective. And the truth is that you would not be hearing this now if things were not just as they are because homo sapiens would have just come to an evolutionary dead end. And truth tell, it lands us men in a lot more trouble than it ever brought on you. So, if you're looking for sympathy about it, please inquire elsewhere.

Rather than be cranky, you should be thankful. If men thought with anything other than their dicks, 98% of them wouldn't give you the time of day. I mean, why would a man pay any attention to you at all were it not for the prospect of boning you? What, your personality? Your companionship? Sharing interests? *Please.*

Let's just get real here, ladies. Think of any time a man has ever bought you dinner, candy, flowers, jewelry, taken you on vacation, paid your bills, carried your crap, repaired your car or fixed any of those other thingies in your life with moving parts that seem to elude your understanding.

Now, take your vagina out of the equation. You can kiss it all goodbye. If you think that isn't true, then look at how men treat each other. Most men have only two words for other men who can't or won't carry their weight entirely. "See ya." That is what not having a vagina will get you from a man.

And let's get even more real. You, of course, already know all this, don't you? That is why you women spend billions of dollars collectively on cosmetics, alluring clothing, fake tits and the like. And before you come across with some tired old, "I do those things for me," bullshit line, just stop. Save that stuff for your girlfriends. They need their delusions reinforced much more than I need my intelligence insulted. You sexualize yourself because it brings you power. Probably the only kind of power you know how to garner.

See, here's the problem. Men thinking with their dicks and your playing that to get ahead has always been a good deal for you. I mean, c'mon, surely you can see that biology has dealt you the "get out of jail and everything else free" card.

Just use it with some class and dignity and it will be passed down to your daughters and their daughters. It's a gift that keeps on giving. Also, you should seriously start thinking about the long-term impact of hypocritically shaming men's natural inclinations, even as you exploit them.

In fact, you can already see the result. Numbers of men, and I mean *growing* numbers, have been so barraged with the shaming that they have started listening to it. Many of them have thought about it and concluded, "Man, they're right! I do think with my dick!"

Ladies, that is not good news for you because the day men quit thinking with their dicks, you are truly fucked. So, my first suggestion to you is to smarten up enough to know a good thing when you see it. And two, use the thing you're most gifted at, self-interest, and see this realistically. I've already covered the material and free labor incentives for embracing the natural order of things but there's another benefit you probably never considered. It can help you keep from becoming so psychotic.

Like so many of the things for which you like to bash men, it requires you to embrace two diametrically opposed sets of beliefs at the same time.

When you're lamenting the men who think with their dicks, yet continue your parasitic exploitation of them, you just end up in a hostile-dependent mindset that leaves you in constant conflict. It may appear that as a woman you can change beliefs as easily as you change your face, but the resultant craziness is unavoidable. And so is the ensuing state of permanent dissatisfaction.

You can't depend on something you hate and ever be happy or completely sane. That fact is just as hard-wired as human sexuality. So, the way I see it, you have three options here. First, as I've been going on about, drop the hate and embrace reality. What comes with that, though, is that you must admit that you, as a woman, are weak and that your worth can be measured by your cup size. Just take your anger about that somewhere other than the men you are counting on to take care of you. They didn't choose human biology any more than you did.

Or, second, you can stay crazy and unhappy. That will be what most of you do and it doesn't deserve another word from me.

Or, finally, and this is for the small percentage of you who can beat the bio-programming, drop the dependency. I know, fat chance, right? Still, it is an option. All it takes is finding your purse when the dinner check arrives, learning how to change a tire and asking for a toolbox instead of jewelry for a birthday present.

I know, it hardly seems romantic. But you may learn that real love is not something a man pulls out of his pocket. And what you may find in going this direction is that the desire to be loved and respected for who you are will quit getting swallowed up by your being an anchor around a man's neck, instead of a grownup partner who adds to his life.

All you must do to get there is to stop thinking with your little brain and start thinking with the big one.

Some Thoughts on Anthony Bourdain

Anthony Bourdain killed himself on the 8th of June 2018. At this point, it's an old story. Just the same, I want to look at what happened in consideration of the information that came to the surface in the days following his death.

I took the position at the time, and still do, that his suicide was primarily a product of being suicidal. Or in other words, he died because he wanted to. That's what truly suicidal people do. No great mystery to unwrap. Well, unless you're one of the nutcases on the internet who are bent on claiming that Bourdain's supposed suicide was a CIA black op conducted on behalf of Hillary Clinton. I have taken the liberty to assume, to hope, that this is the same group of intellectual cripples who claim that school shootings like the one in Florida were also staged by government agents.

The internet is a tree that bears stupid fruit.

Alex Jones worthy conspiracies aside, there is another reason to take a second look at the death of Anthony Bourdain. The story behind it is a worthy one despite the ending, which, as I've already belabored, was a fixed outcome. Anthony Bourdain was bound to take his own life. Driven by some form of clinical depression, life trapped in an anhedonic fog would eventually do him in. He was destined to find a reason to kill himself.

What is interesting to me is that his reason, his personal back-breaking straw, appears to have been a familiar trait in so many men of his ilk. Toxic masculinity. And yes, toxic masculinity is most certainly a thing. It's not the bullshit about men from feminists. That toxic masculinity mostly exists in the warped minds of the gender studies crowd.

Toxic masculinity, the kind I am talking about, is something much more real. And Anthony Bourdain had it in the worst way. In fact, he had such a profoundly toxic sense of his own manhood that it surprises me that it took him almost 62 years to find a crisis that would bring the curtain down on his life.

To understand this, we need to look at the one factor that can reliably tell us how sick a man is. Relationships with women. Because relationships, if you'll pardon the religious reference, are God's way of showing us just how sick we really are.

In the case of Anthony Bourdain, his primary relationship in life was with Asia Argento, an Italian actress with a lot of B-list work. She is also a singer and a feminist activist who levied a claim, 20 years after the supposed fact, that Harvey Weinstein performed oral sex on her against her will.

Uh, yeah. I'm sure that Argento's desire for fame and fortune in Hollywood had nothing to do with her letting a powerful Hollywood producer go down on her. After all, women don't do those things for movie roles, right?

Anyway, twenty years later, Argento made an Oscar-worthy performance of her totally unsubstantiated claim at the Cannes Film Festival. Coincidentally, this was when the #MeToo Movement was gaining traction. In other words, Argento got really brave as soon as there was blood in the water.

This is who Anthony Bourdain fell in love with. And not just in love, but crazy in love. After his death, a Daily Mirror article came out titled "Anthony Bourdain was 'so crazy in love' with girlfriend Asia Argento before suicide that 'friends were worried.'"

It was subtitled, "The intensity of the tragic TV chef's feelings is said to have been a 'red flag' for friends before his suicide." Now, that article uses unnamed sources, which may or may not cast doubts on its authenticity, but Bourdain's well-documented public reaction to Argento's damseling over Harvey Weinstein and the rest of the male world hardly contradicts it.

Bourdain wasn't just a supportive boyfriend standing by his girlfriend as she "fought valiantly for justice." An article in The Independent revealed a streak of sadistic fantasy in Bourdain quite common to toxically masculine men.

"However much people want to see Harvey Weinstein dead or in jail, he's in fucking Arizona," Bourdain said, unable to resist his trademark condescension of American flyover country. "He is in Arizona, eating in restaurants in Arizona. And at off-the-grid restaurants in Arizona, so he can't even eat at the best sushi restaurant in Scottsdale."

"He's gotta go to some shit fucking place," Bourdain continued, "So Arizona, I mean, as much as I'd like to see him, you know beaten to death in his cell."

In addition to his thoughts on Arizona being Weinstein's hell, the article said, "Bourdain also revealed his theory around Weinstein's eventual death – which he imagined would occur in a bathtub."

Picturing him "naked in his famous bathrobe," Bourdain suggested that Weinstein will be brushing his teeth and holding his cellphone when a massive stroke hits him.

Bourdain imagined that Weinstein's life will end, stumbling backward into the bathtub, as the ex-Hollywood producer "scrolls through his contacts list trying to figure out who he can call, who will actually answer the phone."

According to Bourdain, Weinstein dying "knowing that no one will help him" and that he does not look his best, will be fitting.

All this, because Asia Argento claims that Harvey Weinstein forced her to receive oral sex.

One might wonder if, in the fervor of his white knighting, it did not occur to him to ask her what she was doing in Harvey Weinstein's hotel room. Maybe he didn't even wonder what stopped her from getting up and walking out. Was there a gun to her head? A knife? A threat of bodily harm? Where the ever-loving fuck was her agency in any of this?

Was it written out of the script? Or did she just want a movie role bad enough to open her legs for it?

It appears that asking any of these questions wasn't in Bourdain's otherwise considerable skill set. He was too busy donning armor and calling for his trusty steed to bother with the lack of plausibility in Argento's story. But that is hardly surprising for a man whose feelings for the woman was raising red flags among his friends.

Blind infatuation with a woman. The most prolific source of toxic masculinity there is.

It appears that Bourdain's feelings for Argento knew no bounds. Not of reason, nor rationality, nor even of basic human decency. And so, too, were her feelings for him. At least if you take her word for it.

"I am beyond devastated," she tweeted after hearing of his death. "He was my rock."

Perhaps that's true. Perhaps he was her rock. But it appears that while he may have been her rock, he wasn't her cock. At least not exclusively.

In the days just prior to Bourdain's suicide, Argento, 42, was photographed canoodling in public with French reporter, Hugo Clément, 14 years her junior and 33 years younger than Bourdain. Bourdain was on set filming an episode of *Parts Unknown*.

An Italian photographer apparently snapped photos of them in the act and had them online. He reportedly pulled the pics down immediately after news of Bourdain's death broke.

Now, to be fair, there are a lot of parts unknown here. I can't prove that Anthony Bourdain ever saw those pics, or that he heard the truth about Argento cheating on him before deciding to hang himself in his hotel room just 5 days after those photos were taken. I can't prove that his suicide was even remotely connected to his relationship with the #MeToo poser.

I am satisfied, though, that the series of events points to the plausibility of an Argento betrayal of Anthony Bourdain that served as the final straw on his clinically depressed back, leading to his suicide. And I can imagine that with a lot more credibility than any ridiculous notion that it was a black op constructed by the deep state. Least credible is the notion that the day he committed suicide was arbitrary.

Something triggered him to snap, fatally, and my money says it was Argento's knife being plunged through his misguided, chivalrous heart.

It appears very likely from the public record that Anthony Bourdain was crazily, toxically in love with Asia Argento, who cheated on him publicly while they were separated by work. That served as his reward for loving her; for the fake gallantry of white knighting for someone who was ultimately just out for one more ride on the cock carousel.

For all his vengeful fantasies and sadistic ideations about Harvey Weinstein's death, it is Anthony Bourdain who is dead in the ground. He met his untimely end in the bathroom of his hotel room with the belt of a bathrobe, eerily like the way he imagined Harvey Weinstein dying. He didn't even have the luxury of being sentenced to life in Arizona.

I hope, as always in life, that there is more here than just an opportunity to look smugly upon the foolishness of blue pill men. That at the very least their folly at life serves the larger lesson.

Surely, Anthony Bourdain is dead because he had a malady of thinking, of perceiving life that diminished its importance to him. That is a formidable thing to oppose, both for the victim and the society around them.

But what is also apparent here is that for all his creative genius, his uncanny capacity to step outside of himself and shape a story about people and places in this world, he could not apply those gifts to himself. He could not see himself, even for a moment, outside the gynocentric mold. He invested everything, down to his very identity, in a woman, and he inevitably choked on it.

I don't feel smug in the least saying this. There's no gloating here. Just gratitude that there are ways to elude the tragedy that Anthony Bourdain couldn't. And I hope that anyone contemplating this bad ending is able to see that the ability of a man to reimagine himself, away from all this gynocentric madness, this toxic masculinity that perverts and degrades the self, may also bear the ability to beat back the demon of depression; to restore and revitalize not only the will to live, but the determination to do so with passion.

A Prayer for Joe Bob

Seeing his reflection in the lives of all the lonely men who reach for anything they can to keep from going home. ~ Kris Kristofferson

Joe Bob searches his home futilely for a place to store a box of baseball cards he's collected since childhood. Everywhere he looks is already packed to the edges with something else. The bedroom closets, all four of them, are choked with enough clothing and shoes to start an eBay business. The closets in the hallway are equally spoken for, stacked chin level with cardboard boxes much like the one he's holding, except they haven't been opened in a generation.

With a sigh he lumbers to the garage and wedges the box in a corner, feeling the sides buckle a little as he forces it between his fishing gear and some power tools. Back inside, something starts to claw at him somewhere in the pit of his stomach, like talons sinking into a small animal. It was the trip to the garage. It was a little too…familiar.

There were two things that all of the closets had in common. One, as you know, they were all full. Two, almost none of that stuff was Joe Bob's. Between wife and kids, his home was fully occupied. And it wasn't just the closets. Everything from bathroom counters to bookshelves to the basement was the terrain of others. What remained for him was trying to squeeze in what little he had around the property of those considered to actually live there.

Joe Bob's heart sank with an intractable sense of the walls closing in around him. It was as though he had become the baseball cards, stuffed into a cardboard coffin and shoved in the corner with no room to breathe. It wasn't just a shortage of space. It was something much more personal; more important.

He thought about the fishing gear. If he were to use it again, he'd have to replace all the line. By now it was brittle with age and neglect. Somewhere along the way, exactly when long forgotten, the fishing trips just ended. They had been shelved with other childish things that interfered with his duties to provide for a family. His wife was instrumental in helping this along. Any mention he made of fishing, or any personal enjoyment, was met with cold disapproval and not so subtle questioning of his priorities. The few times he didn't cave into that he paid for with guilt being tied around his neck like a noose. Eventually, he got the point. He might go fishing, but he wasn't going to be allowed to enjoy it.

As time passed by, so did life in a way. Friends slipped away, personal interests and hobbies became memories. The lack of personal space became a lack of personal identity. Somewhere between the early days and where he stood now his life had morphed into something defined only by automated compliance with the needs, and frequently whims, of others. Eventually, he reached a place where he could barely remember that he liked fishing to begin with. He wasn't sure he could remember liking anything at all.

Not that there wasn't an abundance of rewards from taking care of his family. He loved his family; would lay down in traffic for them. In the end, though, robotic caretaking leaves a lot to be desired. Ask any woman. Rebelling from it is inviting a firestorm into your home. Ask any man.

As you probably know, Joe Bob is an imaginary friend. Rather he is a composite of a lot of men I have known. And while the character is fictional, his story is not. It's a story not often told, much less in mixed company.

Contrary to popular worldview, men feel. They feel as deeply and profoundly as any woman. If you peel back a man's skin, you find flesh and blood, not gears and wires. Men have wants, needs, desires and dreams outside their role as protectors and providers. They are not whole without these things and yet they all too often surrender them without so much as a struggle.

Many men are Joe Bob; working to provide, complaining little about their lot in life and sacrificing much for the sake of those they love. But sooner or later something gives. It always does.

Joe Bob is average as far as men go. Likely as not he can't really identify and articulate why the world seems like it is closing in around him. It just is. He doesn't know that standing up to his wife and insisting she supports his taking time for his own interests might solve the problem, or at least lessen it. If he thinks of it at all, he knows such an effort would only result in heated conflict and fishing gear gathering more dust in the corner of his garage.

So, he reaches for stuff. He does it without exactly knowing why. A bottle, drugs, violence, even another woman. Anything to feel alive again. He is reaching for the wrong things for the right reasons.

I am not excusing Joe Bob or trying to say that this explains the worst to be found in some men. I am saying that it might indeed explain some of it. And it surely needs an explanation. For when all the things Joe Bob reaches for ultimately fail him, he sometimes reaches for a gun. This isn't a blanket explanation of suicide. Nor would any one thing explain it so simply. But I do know this: People who take their own lives often feel like they are alone.

Joe Bob doesn't feel like he is alone, he is unshakably certain of it.

A Tribute to Uncle Walter

This is just a snip from the early days, not as the victim of the forces that diminish the lives of men but as a co-conspirator and accomplice in the problem. PE

I had a perchance meeting as a very young man. I guess I was about 12 or 13. I was with my parents visiting my Aunt Johnnie. Her house, an aging retreat built from rough-hewn stones in all manner of shapes and sizes, was a regular stop for my family. We gathered there, especially on Sunday afternoons when she, still wearing her church clothing, made loaves of fresh bread. The kitchen radiated her works, filling her home and my head with that wondrous aroma. The feeling of family hung in the air alongside the scent of a bakery. There were usually other members of my extended family there, drawn with appetites and smiles to the same location.

I remember one day walking from the kitchen through the house, just poking around the empty rooms, having tired of the adults. I passed into a bedroom where there was a man lying on the bed. He looked up at me without expression. It was my Uncle Walter.

He looked aged and withered; on the verge of broken. Lines covered the whole of his face, revealing a man who was tired beyond the simple meaning of the word. I could tell he had been working; doing something hard. I knew, though why I knew still escapes me, that he was doing something that was sucking the life out of him.

He just lay there on the bed looking at me. He neither smiled nor scowled. His face was neither welcoming nor menacing. Even in the road map of his time-worn brow and cheeks there was an emotional flatness. He would have seemed to be a dead man were it not for the gentle rising and falling of his exposed belly underneath his shirt.

He simply stared at me, revealing nothing of who he was or whatever thoughts were hiding behind his uncurious blue eyes.

I stood there transfixed, knowing this was my uncle, but recognizing that I knew nothing about him. We were visiting my aunt, after all, not this shell of a man laying alone in a bedroom. Even today I scarcely remember anything about him other than that moment.

And as to that moment, for some reason it frightened me. *He* frightened me. My gaze wandered to the floor. Then I quickly scurried out, finding anywhere else to be.

The next memory I have is that of his funeral. My Aunt Johnnie was wailing openly, a relative at each of her elbows, holding her up.

It would be fifty years before it dawned on me that I was more moved by her grief than I was the loss of my uncle. It would take still more time for me to realize the sadness of that and the shame in me it represented.

So many invisible men, buried in life by the unending work that defines their worth; buried in back rooms by loved ones and families as they go about baking and eating the bread those men provide. Buried in death by those they supported and cared for.

And then buried from memory by the likes of me.

I have not taken a moment to think about my Uncle Walter, one of the many men I never knew. He's scarcely crossed my mind since the day one possible, frightening version of me lay in solitude on a deathbed while the kitchen was alive with food and family. All this in a home he built but in which some ways he was not allowed to belong.

Whoever you were, Uncle Walter, wherever you are, please know that I am looking back at you now and I see you.

Women

Princess Miserable and the Great American Bitch Machine

I need to start, without hesitation, by tipping my hat to women who stand by their men in sickness and in health, no matter what might befall them in life. I also acknowledge women who work, contribute equally to their relationship lives in terms of finance and make some sort of effort to carry their weight in other ways, like say, getting out of a car to help change a flat tire – or finding a reasonable *compromise* to a conflict in their relationships.

There, I've said it. There are indeed some good, no, *great* women in the world. I've even met some of them. Now, however, I need to spend my time addressing women that most of the men in the world must deal with in real life, especially as they get a little older.

This won't be popular with some. Straight talk about real women, regardless of age, has a strange effect on the indoctrinated, blue pill world. Just check out some of the reactions from the feminists, the mainstream media and even some traditionalists to anyone who stands up and speaks the truth about the sexes. The last 10 years of my life has been inundated with daggers being thrown from the pearl-clutching lot of them.

It's quite comical to read about it online. You can almost just see them, spittle flying over their keyboards as they hammer away in angry spastic fits, like manic Daffy Ducks on methamphetamine.

"Sthee! Stheeeee!! Ith's Mithogyny! MITH-O-GYN-EEE! He just hateths women!"

Well, no I don't. I don't hate children either, but I sometimes find them annoying, largely for the same reasons I am annoyed by a lot of women. Take that back, it is for *exactly* the same reasons. There is really no difference at all, except that if I say anything corrective about women, I become *The Grinch Who Stole Valentine's Day* in the eyes of society; a modern day Snidely Whiplash, standing over poor, defenseless Nell, tied to the train tracks while I snicker and twirl my moustache.

Enough of digressing into my troubles. It's time for a story. I was doing a cross-country trip many years back, in my trucking days. I had the CB on, trying to make time and avoid cops, and was listening to a conversation between two truckers; both sounded like they were middle-aged or thereabouts. One was telling the other about how he kept a travel bag ready by the door every time he went home so that when the nagging and disharmony his wife created became too much to bear, he could just pick up that bag and head right back on the road with no preparation at all.

An instant escape plan; one apparently that he had used a few times over the years.

The other driver said he understood perfectly well and then wondered aloud in the creative phrasing I'd come to expect from my fellow drivers, "I never could figure 'em out. A woman would rather climb over a barbed wire fence and crawl through cactus and cow shit to start a fight than to just look you in the eye and solve a problem."

Then another truck driver chimed in out of nowhere to the conversation on the radio.

"That's because they're all children." he said, "Every last goddam one of them."

The radio fell into a silence that spoke volumes. Not another word needed to be said. Indeed, none was.

Now it is easy, obligatory for many and compulsive for others to conjure up a reflexive "blue pill" interpretation of the conversation; to boil it down to some dismissive charge of woman-hating.

The only problem is that there is a lot of truth in everything that was said.

We do have, for several reasons, a pandemic of gross immaturity in western women. I just heard a few duck feathers ruffle – which means the squawking is not far off, but if the pussy police are coming for me, I might as well finish what I started.

The problem begins with fairy tales; Prince Charming to the rescue, mystical unicorns and the like. It gets solid reinforcement from the "daddy" component of the "daddy's little girl" equation and turns into a lifelong fantasy by many women which means a rich, handsome male supporter, lots of fulfilled whims and eternal adulation for being beautiful, *or for just being*. All this comes with a commensurate lack of expectation that our porcelain princess will need to contribute anything to a relationship but her looks, an occasional blowjob and a wish list from Tiffany's.

Now, all this would seem easy enough to fix. Such unhealthy fantasies should be dispelled right around the time we tell children there is no Santa Claus, Tooth Fairy or Easter Bunny. We could tell little girls that when sexual maturity approaches, they need to "woman up."

But something else happens.

Daddy continues to treat his little girl like a princess, thus creating and reinforcing her future expectations of men. Mom often augments that with bitch lessons. And together we set about, with every form and force in the culture, to help women build and maintain a comprehensive collection of childish beliefs about themselves.

We give them "Princess" t-shirts and tiaras instead of the truth and a moral compass. And they wear that commercialized princess gear far, far past the point of reason. Often, they wear it to the grave, even if just in their minds. They never know that to the mature mind they look like a middle-aged man with a plastic superhero's mask on, ringing a doorbell and shouting, "Trick or Treat!" in a high-pitched squeal on Halloween night.

There is just something awfully wrong with that picture. But they don't see it at all. They have socially enabled blindness to their own ridiculousness, and they don't much care for anyone shining a light on it. The worst of it for women is that it sets up a pattern of perpetual disappointment and frustration that is the hallmark of so many women's lives. You can't satisfy the insatiable, and trying is insanity, but that is exactly what women expect from men. And it is what a lot of men try haplessly to do, making the problem all the worse.

Even before most women's looks start to fade, many of them are shocked to find out that Prince Charming is human after all, and that, surprisingly, he gets a little tired of being held to her royal expectations.

Of course, that means there is something wrong with *him*. So, our western woman embarks on the path of countless numbers of her sisters. She dumps her Prince Charming, cranks up the insanely demanding volume, and goes in search of a non-defective "man unit."

The self-help and women's magazine industry are quite tuned in to this, so they run constant "How to Get a Man to___ (fill in the blank with childish desire du jour)" articles. They do this knowing that there are literally millions of women readers who have just fired that last disappointing bastard.

They have not figured out that their relationship problems are in the mirror and with the help of all those who profit from such ignorance, they are not going to.

Then, despite having a better standard of living and more options than any human beings in history, they get even more miserable. After all, compulsive shopping has been tried, and tried, and tried. Seems that rampant consumerism won't erase the lines on your face or defy the force of gravity. So, it fails, and women got even more depressed. The glitter on their "Proud Bitch" t-shirts starts falling off.

Enter the pharmaceutical companies. Sometimes a failure to mature and develop reasonable expectations must be addressed chemically. It is the prescription version of COSMO, ostensibly meant to treat depression but it's prescribed for a deficit of maturity and accountability.

Women's taste for anti-depressants now rivals their taste for chocolate. Find me one woman over 40 who has never been on antidepressants and I will show you a woman with no health insurance. All this too, of course, is our defective Prince Charming's fault. Just ask your average feminist. Men are at the root of all these problems. They must be because women aren't allowed to have problems of their own making.

It seems that women are generally in one of two states these days. They are either trying desperately to make themselves into what will attract the imaginary Sir Galahads, or they are immersed in bitterness because they have finally figured out that Sir Galahad can only be found in storybooks. Or, as so many women are wont to do, they are doing both at the same time, alternating between childish fantasy and their thirst for revenge on men who can't make that fantasy become real. Hell, even men who try their damnedest to fill that role can't keep it up. It's just too much work. And let's face it. A six-year-old inhabiting the body of a grown woman isn't worth it.

It seems to me that if women simply matured and developed reasonable expectations of men, *as well as themselves*, the bell might toll for COSMO, the entire self-help industry, the cosmetic industry, the cosmetic surgery industry, 99% of all psychotherapists and at least 10 very lucrative psychoactive drugs.

Oh, and they might find some happiness with themselves and with men who don't have to jump through stupid hoops to try to make them happy.

No, wait a minute. That can't be. If all that were true then that would mean that women, as a class are being duped out of countless billions of dollars of their (and their men's) money, year after year, either on the pursuit of a childish pipe dream, or their anger over what should be its obvious unattainability.

It would mean that all these entities, feminism, consumer products, psychology, media, advertising, politics and social custom had all merged into one Great Big Bitch Machine. It would mean that the modern female psyche is nothing more than a product of that machine. And it would mean that the woman attached to that psyche now has to go out to work a shitty job so she can buy and consume other products of that very machine or get some man to do it for her.

And it would explain why the quality of her life and her happiness deteriorates with every passing year.

Nah, that can't be. Just ask any feminist. It's all because we live in a patriarchy.

Women's Sexual Peak Sits on a Pile of Lies

Some years ago, I was at a night club with a group of men and women. Naturally, the conversation turned to sex. One woman, in her late forties, said, in a good-natured way, "It's a shame that by the time men really learn what they are doing in bed, their equipment doesn't work like it used to."

"I understand how you feel," I said, in an equally jovial tone, "By the time women start learning what they are doing in bed, their looks have faded."

My response, while as truthful as hers, took her out of the conversation. It was not my intent at all, but you could tell by the look in her eyes that she felt like every line on her face was magnified a thousand times, reading like a giant "use by" date from the last millennium. Fortunately for me, I didn't have all manner of ego and identity tied up in my penis, or I might have felt the same way.

There was a silver lining, though. It did spark a rather lively round of verbal sparring with the rest of the people at the table. And I'm sure that it was a discussion that has been echoed millions of times at millions of night club gatherings.

Why is it that men and women hit their sexual peaks at such radically different ages?

And the answer is, of course, that they don't. It is just another one of the countless lies we enable women to live for the sake of not disturbing their self-image.

Where else but the current gender zeitgeist can a woman with crow's feet, sagging breasts, reduced sexual hormones, a vagina that does not lubricate as it once did, and less ability to attract sexual partners of their preference, stand up and say, "I am in my sexual prime," and have everyone in their presence nod their head in agreement?

Only in a world where we tell women whatever they want to hear, no matter how ridiculous. In other words, the world we live in.

And it admittedly fits with part of women's experience to maintain the lie. An observation I have, one that I cannot back up with any research, is that as women's biological clocks tick down toward the final moments, there is a tendency, in the words of Dylan Thomas, to *rage against the dying of the light.*

It's not sexual primacy, it's desperate horniness. Their fantasy of being in their sexual prime when they are well past it is only the labored breathing of someone in their last moments, struggling to suck air just a little while longer.

I am not knocking it. When I was 21, I had a 45-year-old woman show me *what fer, good and proper,* for three weeks in a cabin in Oklahoma. It was an educational rite of passage and a very fond memory in my life. Wouldn't trade it for the world.

But, let's face it, the only one in that cabin in their sexual prime was me. I was a youngster with a gold mine of a horny older woman desperate for sexual relevance. And when the experience was over, I walked away smiling, and a little better equipped to take care of business with women who were in their sexual prime.

And she had at least one more round of clinging to her sexual power; to her relevance in the world.

The point is that without sexual viability, the power of most women in this culture is reduced to whatever is afforded by rote chivalry. And while that chivalry affords them a great deal of latitude, it doesn't provide them with the meaningful significance of a younger woman who still turns heads - *and can have babies.*

Being in your sexual prime is about being ready to make babies, not about how willing you are to play bronco for a young cowboy.

In the purely biological sense, infertile women, even those that just appear to be, are just so much excess baggage. And since women as a group either cannot or will not draw their self-worth from anything but sexual power, we will forever have them demanding to live lies. And in modern times, they even have the option of paying surgeons to cut, suction and inject that lie until it looks damn near the truth.

Business is booming.

There is a solution to this, though it is doubtful we will ever get there.

Women have long lamented the male beauty standard, even as they apply makeup with a trowel. They claim it drives women to extremes like surgery and eating disorders and results in damaged self-esteem, all because men want women to look a certain way.

But of course, once you peel back the layers of victim-drivel and get to the core of the matter, you find that women drive themselves to do these things, biology leading them by the nose, because beauty is their quickest route to personal power, and because they don't rise above the raw biology and find relevance in other ways.

Like men do.

When women collectively quit worrying about sexual primacy and start focusing on their own innate human potential, when they learn to value their own accomplishments more than they value what they can sexually manipulate out of men, the plastic surgeons will go out of business and their bad self-esteem, rather than their personal significance, will be facing expiration.

What's that you say, women already are like that? They already do more on their own than they try to get men to do for them through sex and other forms of manipulation?

Well, I would like to address that here, too. But I only take on one lie at a time.

Daddy's Little Nightmare

I've had many, many conversations over the years with regular men about some highly irregular ideas. Interestingly, most of the men I've talked to have been open to the discussions. My observations about men, women and the behavior typical to both resonated with them. I've routinely found men nodding agreeably as I described some of their not-so-positive experiences with women. They did so even as some of them instinctively glanced over their shoulder as if to make sure no one was seeing them agree with me.

Plenty of them even quietly acceded to my calling them out on their tendency to tolerate abuse, to appease some despicably behaving women in order to stay out of the doghouse. It's common to a lot of men; a life spent in some measure of frustration, trying to placate an errant child, jumping through hoops to keep a fragile peace. Sure, some men don't share this experience. And some men claim they don't. You can hear them bragging about how they lord over their relationships -- when the woman isn't listening. But most men I have talked to who are in relationships identify with the role of enabler to one degree or another.

Most of them can chuckle at themselves a little bit when they talk about how they put up with the childish demands and entitled attitudes of their female counterparts. Some of them, without compunction, even cast themselves metaphorically as powerless little schoolboys, fearful of being sent to the principal's office, represented by the disapproval of their wives or girlfriends. They do this with no sense of embarrassment, as though they think all men live this way. And of course, there are plenty of men who do.

All this introspective honesty, this good-natured self-disclosure, takes a nosedive, however, when I've talked to men as fathers, vs just husbands or boyfriends. In that matter things become, shall we say, pricklier.

You see, it's easy for a man to admit that petulant childishness is the default setting for a good many "grown" women. Most men will just nod their heads knowingly and shrug it off because, in their minds, that's just the way women are.

It's quite another matter when you start to talk about the role of fathers in instilling said petulance and childishness; when you acknowledge that "daddy's little girl" is highly prone to grow up (or just get older) and become "daddy's insatiable little bitch," or much worse.

It's quite ironic, listening to a man complain about how his wife has crazy unreal expectations. He bemoans the fact that she cannot be satisfied no matter what he does. He claims that he pulls his hair out trying to figure out how to satisfy her endless demands only to be met with more disapproval and, of course, more demands. He wonders aloud how she ever learned to be such a bottomless pit of needs and also such a bitch about it.

Then you watch him interact with his four-year-old daughter, whom he will endlessly coddle and for whom he will go to any measure to make sure she's never denied even the most trivial of whims and that she never faces even the most remote of consequences for her actions.

Former vice-president Joe Biden once talked about being routinely physically abused by his older sister, informing the world that his parents would have "gone nuclear" if he had ever defended himself. Those were the family rules, and they were not negotiable. The girl got to inflict physical pain on the other children with impunity. The boys got to take it. As Biden recounted, "I've got the bruises to prove it."

My experience informs me that the Bidens weren't by any means the only family who operated on the premise that assault was permissible by girls, and self-defense by boys was forbidden.

That four-year-old girl doesn't grow out of it. It continues as she turns five. And fifteen, and twenty-five. And as she ages the father takes on a role with abundant Freudian implications, acting as a sexual guardian over her life; a sentinel inspecting every boy who shows interest. He measures up each potential suitor for whether he can emulate the father's indulgent enabling of his little princess. And his presence infers possible physical retribution for non-hackers and those who cross lines. When it comes to turning human females into paragons of pissy entitlement, the western father has few rivals. Daddy's little girl has daddy wrapped around her little finger.

Has anyone ever coined a phrase describing how a son has a parent wrapped around his little finger? Of course not, because it largely doesn't happen. The closest thing you'll ever hear to that is the term "Mama's Boy" which is an entirely different story.

"Mama's Boy" implies blind service to the mother. It is a pejorative pointing to the general weakness of the son and the power of the mother. Having daddy wrapped around your little finger implies just the opposite. It is the raw sexual power of the female, and the powerlessness of the father, even with daughter in the state of childhood. She can just crawl into daddy's lap, wrap her little arms around his neck and get her way, every time. He just melts. I will spare us all an analysis of the psychosexual implications of that little scenario. It's too gross to go into. Suffice it to say that both family scenarios involve females with power and males without it.

Fathers, in this regard, generally don't take well to a discussion of the subject. I've talked to several of them about enabling dads who treat their little girls like princesses, effectively turning them into obnoxious cunts who are destined to make a succession of men completely miserable, and who will, in the end, be miserable themselves. Nobody can hold on to any kind of happiness when happiness hinges on chronic, insanely unrealistic expectations. That's the curse of modern womanhood. It's why so many of them are miserable, and why they feel justified in making others miserable when they are inevitably disappointed.

Now, at some point in the conversations with a handful of these fathers, they seemed to reach a snapping point. "Wait a minute," they'd say, in a suddenly serious and demanding tone, "You're not talking about me and my daughter, are you?" They weren't kidding.

"Why, not at all," I've lied, aware that I was getting into dangerous territory.

Here I was talking to guys who were so irrational about their little princesses that they looked to be willing to go fisticuffs with a 6'8" 280-pound man if he got too close to the truth.

There is a great deal that goes into creating a society of women who feel so entitled to unrealistic demands of men that they make themselves and everyone else suffer.

Certainly, as I mentioned earlier, feminism has played a huge role in this. So have obsequious, spineless men. The kind of men who never met a woman they wouldn't bend over backward to please. There's also basic biology. Men are driven to scatter seeds and most of them want and need women's permission and approval to do it. That alone has them urging women toward very unrealistic expectations in the long term. Very few men can maintain the lengths they go through to achieve sexual conquest. We hear women complain about that all the time when Sir Galahad was granted access to the bedroom, only to turn into a frog after he'd had his fill of filling her.

Indeed, as we look at all of this from the aerial view, we see that men, in one form or another, are the main culprits. It's entirely arguable that feminists are only demanding of men what they know men will ultimately give them, reasonable or not. So, in that light, the sole enablers of all this nonsense are men.

That includes fathers.

Fathers are the first arena where women learn their expectations of men. Fathers are the gateway to hypergamy and gynocentrism. They are women's first lessons in all-take, no-give relationships, and where they begin to learn the sheer awesomeness of their sexual power.

Consider that the next time you see a father walking hand in hand with a little girl wearing a tiara and a t-shirt with the word "Princess" written in glitter across the front. Think of it when you hear a teenage girl gush about all the things her daddy buys for her, or when you hear a father boast that "nothing's too good for my little girl," when they would not dream of saying the same about their sons.

Think about it a little more when you see entire families enable abusive girls; when their relational and other forms of aggression flourish at the expense of everyone else, particularly the boys.

And if you ever wonder why corrupt, disingenuous ideologies of privilege, like feminism, are so warmly received by a generation of females who think entitlement is the natural order of things, then take a deeper look at how they got there.

If you are looking clearly, you'll see that chivalrous fathers are a big part of the problem. They create a breeding ground for feminists and narcissists. And they will indeed get angry, possibly violent when you call them out on it.

So, in most cases, it's better to just let it be. There's nothing to be gained by standing between daddy and his Little Nightmare. Just make sure you don't make the same mistake so many men do - by picking up where daddy left off.

A Primer on Hypergamy

Hypergamy. The word is part of the common vernacular of the manosphere, though you'll find precious few people in the mainstream who know what it means. And, however obscure its meaning may be to the average person, for the community of men daring to see themselves outside the box, it is a very important idea to understand.

Defined literally, it is not very complicated. Hypergamy means marrying up; marrying into a higher social or financial class. It's an obscure word considering that it is the objective of about 98% of women in this society who want to marry. It's counterpart word, hypogamy, describes women who marry down, beneath their means. All three of them.

That's the basics. However, it is best to look past the literal definition and use an expanded understanding of hypergamy to describe a range of behavioral traits that point to the natural inclination of women to pair bond their way into a better life. Hypergamy, when we are thinking from the neck up, is a constant reminder of what we are confronted with in women. Hopefully, in the fog of sexual attraction and emotional infatuation, it helps us to see women's proclivities and motivations more clearly.

It's important to note here that hypergamy, in the Red Pill definition, is about a lot more than money and personal power. And by that, I mean it is about a lot more than what a woman is attracted to in men and who she is inclined to marry because women don't just marry up, they also *fuck* up. They lean, not just toward a bigger home, or nicer clothes, but to better action in the sack than you can get after having sex with the same person 2,000 times. And, true to hypergamous tendencies, they are not inclined to pay for any of it. In the realm of sociobiology, that points to cuckoldry as a manifestation of hypergamy.

Allow me to mansplain this. A woman finds herself a nice doctor or lawyer. He works hard, brings home the bacon, treats her with respect, doesn't hit her, drink excessively, gamble money away or cheat on her. Most men, including those who pride themselves on having a good understanding of women, will look at this situation and see a woman disinclined toward infidelity. After all, she has it completely made. She comes from a good family. She has an abundant, even cushy home life, generous income that he works for, everything she could ever want all the way down to a massive walk-in closet full of clothes. No way she would cheat, right?

Wrong.

Women are most commonly driven to marry this kind of man for the security he can provide, not because he is what women desire sexually. To be fair, many women will, in fact, restrain the desires fueled by sexual hypergamy. Many will not, though, and this is how the cuckhold is created. Because for many, many women, it's alpha fucks and beta bucks.

The New York Times reveals that 30% of married men who pursue paternity testing find out they are not the biological father of the children they've been told are theirs. Think about that. 30%. Nearly 1/3 of all men who suspect something is rotten on the home front turn out to be right. And what about all the men who never suspect and never test? Are we really to imagine that the only cuckoldry going on is in the men who wise up and start digging into the genetics?

What kind of calamity would ensue right now if every father in the world sought confirmation of their paternity? How many men would we find are going into offices, climbing behind the wheels of semis, driving the streets in squad cars and walking into coal mines every day to pay for the care of offspring that are not their progeny? How many men are now divorced, taking what is left of their paychecks after the courts garnish them into poverty, all for a child or children they did not father?

And that is just the financial consequences. *The Times Magazine* article cited playwright August Strindberg, who explored this topic well over a hundred years ago. And I quote from the article here: "The Father" is the story of a cavalry captain whose wife hints that he might not be the father of the daughter he adores. Consumed with doubt, he rages at his wife: "I have worked and slaved for you, your child, your mother, your servants . . . because I thought myself the father of your child. This is the commonest kind of theft, the most brutal slavery. I have had 17 years of penal servitude and have been innocent."

As a side note, I really appreciated that Strindberg's protagonist even recognized that *he was indentured to the servants of the house* as much as he was to the family who resided there.

Hail patriarchy.

Thirty percent, guys. *30 percent!* And all because women are wired to better deal themselves with anything that has to do with the men in their lives.

Hypergamy plays a role in sending women outside their marriages for more sexually exciting adventures. And as many of you know, the psychological underpinnings of that tendency in women is part of reproductive strategy. Women are wired to reproduce. The drive in them to snag security, money, and power through men are just expressions of the same basic biology.

While I am not a rigid determinist (and don't have much patience for them), you can't deny the role of biology in leading women to select powerful, successful men who can provide enough protection and provision. This is beneficial to long-lasting reproductive success. In the same light, once that protection and provision have been corralled and controlled, it still makes sense that women would seek out and mate with physically superior male specimens, and even be willing to allow the duped dad to believe a big fat lie if it serves her biological mandate.

More telling information is hidden in plain view in marriage statistics. The average marriage lasts 8 years. Couples tend to wait a minimum of two years before having children. That points to the possibility that most divorces are initiated shortly after children start school, when the mother suddenly finds she has a lot more time on her hands, and just as the father's income is starting to reach its peak.

Now, as I often try to point out, none of this is stated to demonize women. Men have their own biological peccadillos, including some number of men who are married and keep producing children with women to whom they are not married. All moral judgments aside, men who lean toward viewing women through the rose-colored glasses of romantic love, which is most of them, tend to remain clueless until the DNA results are in.

And that is if they are both smart and fortunate enough to get the test. As Carnell Smith of Paternityfraud.com informed us about France at the International Conference on Men's Issues in Detroit, 2014: "DNA should mean Do Not Ask. Because it is now illegal to even get a test and if you get a test without the mother's permission you will be criminally prosecuted. And it is not that the test even matters in most cases. There are 36 states in the US that won't relieve duped dads of child support even if they can prove the child is not theirs."

To me, this is more evidence of the biological impetus behind hypergamy. It is a force strong enough to have resulted in state-sanctioned cuckoldry. Women want to better deal themselves. We stand by and let it happen. Quite often we pay for it.

One area where hypergamy seems to fail is in the realm of employment. We have the evidence to support that in the form of an earnings gap between men and women.

Women tend not to negotiate salaries very well, and I speculate that this is because they don't have to. As a group, they get most of what they need from men. Consequently, they develop skills in exploitation and manipulation, not in direct negotiation. In fact, there is some evidence to suggest that the more women earn the less their reproductive chances. It may literally provide women a motive to devalue their worth in employment.

Instead of obsessing on earning, as men do, women operate in the social paradigm that puts the financial onus on men. They do it through divorce and they do it through cuckoldry. Hypergamy drives all of it.

Of course, what you do with this information is up to you. I've personally never let it drive me into isolation, but I don't have any harsh words for men who go that route. Whatever you do, guys, don't be part of the 30% or in the unknown quantity of men who will never know. Don't let yourself forget that hypergamy is real and that it applies to whatever woman is in your life. Exceptions are exceedingly rare. Act accordingly.

Hypergamy and the Power of Women

"When you are married, you might as well wake up every morning, go look at yourself in the mirror and say, "Fuck you. Fuck your dreams, your ambitions and anything else that is important to you. It's all about her." ~ *Chris Rock*

In our efforts to understand and quantify women's power, we are hobbled by the fact that our culture has very limited ways to articulate the nature of that power. In fact, we live largely in denial of the massive amount of muscle and sway inherent to being female, and are under any number of cultural pressures, reinforced by massive societal denial, to act as though that power does not exist.

What would seem to be a minor example of this at work can be seen every time your spellchecker redlines the word misandry, likewise gynocentrism. Though this is not so minor. A culture that refuses to acknowledge that a perfectly legitimate word exists on paper is in effect denying its existence to the collective consciousness. And when such prejudicial elimination of ideas runs unchecked, it not only has the power to skew attitudes and perspectives but also to shape law and policy, education and public awareness. Misandry runs rampant because misandry does not exist.

Women need empowerment, and always will, because women's power itself *does not exist.*

We do have one exception to this. It is the "I am woman, hear me roar" exception. We are bound as members of this society to proclaim women to be powerful, capable equals to men, even as we are also shackled to the opinion that women are the subjugated victims of oppression by the men who they are supposedly equal to. In its own ironic and completely contradictory way, the "I am woman" exception is just a publicly mandated, schmaltzy affirmation of the Stuart Smalley variety. We are all compulsory *grrl power* cheerleaders, chanting therapeutic mantras at women about a kind of power they do not and never have possessed.

And it only serves to lead us further astray from the very real power that they do possess.

We don't have common expressions like "female dominance," or "matriarchal oppression," and despite their absolute legitimacy, as sure as we use them 98% of the public will roll their eyes in summary dismissal, thus demonstrating another aspect of overarching female power that bears no name, and therefore *does not exist.*

It is like trying to describe a cloud without being able to use the word itself - *to a world that does not believe in clouds.* We are limited to talking around the subject; we present our meanings in metaphors and similes and anecdotes. We may describe how the power of accusation from women often ruins innocent men, or how men are disadvantaged in family courts, but we really have **precious little language** to address all this directly. As a result, much of what we say is dismissed as hyperbolic and overly reactionary.

It's the female advantage to have power that is at once overbearing and invisible; everywhere and nowhere.

But this is beginning to change, thanks to the Red Pill. Growing numbers of men are now aware of misandry, despite their spellcheckers' continued ignorance. And with the furtherance of the use of that word, we are not only pushing another addition to the lexicon but some very key ideas that go with it.

- Women can and do, irrationally hate every bit as much as men.
- Women can be sexist, and many are.
- Men can be self-hating, and many are.

That is the power of a single word, and the more it is forced into mainstream use, the more, albeit slowly, that attitudes will begin to change. We are not there yet, but the day is coming that misandry will take its place alongside misogyny in the collective consciousness, and people will have a hard time thinking of one without thinking of the other. Language is the locus of social change.

In that spirit, we are focusing on not only reversing the polarity of the power flow between men and women but on attempting to infuse some more meaning and clarity into the language we use when doing it.

And I can best start by taking a word that has been popping up in our dialog for some time now.

Hypergamy.

The word is literally defined as the custom of women marrying up or marrying men who have a higher socioeconomic status than the women who marry them. We have already expanded on it to describe women's natural inclination to be sexually stimulated in the presence of powerful men. I read a recent comment in another forum saying that even the most committed of married women will get aroused, aka the 'gina tingle, in the presence of such men, even when ugly-ass Henry Kissinger walks into a room.

But there is much more to hypergamy, and at the very least it serves the purpose of men well to revise and expand upon our understanding and include that into our common language.

First, we should consider that the literal definition of hypergamy and the Red Pill definition both point to the same outcome - women with access to, and use of, the power generated by men.

That power can come in many different forms and will be pursued differently by different women, especially at different points in their lives.

A younger woman may be attracted to the immediate presence of personal power via thug attraction, as we see with young, poor women attracted to gang members. All while a more sophisticated woman will be turned on by a successful man of means. There is, in the biological sense, not one iota of difference between the two women. Both get hot and bothered by what they hope to eventually have control over.

So, whether the 'gina tingle is sparked by a guy on a Harley or a guy with a Harley factory, they are tingling over essentially the same thing.

Both women will enter the relationship in the honeymoon phase but will eventually use the tried and tested methods of sexual manipulation and/or emotional blackmail to put the man on a leash and start assuming ownership of everything he produces, including money, home and personal time.

The average woman will become increasingly demanding and insistent that the energy all revolve around her, and the standard response is for the man to acquiesce. And as I wrote about in "A Prayer for Joe Bob," this is where we also see the man lose more and more of himself to her wishes and whims.

Women don't just marry up. They are on constant alert to *better deal* themselves, even within, *especially* within, their current relationships. They enter relationships with the intent to eventually exert total control over them. I saw a woman wearing a t-shirt once that said it as succinctly as I have ever seen it.

"More me. Less you."

To illustrate the point further I am reminded of one of the questions I used to ask in the men's groups I facilitated.

"How many of you," I would ask, "have ever had the feeling that you wanted to pull all of your hair out by the roots and scream bloody murder because no matter what you did, she was not happy with it and wanted more?"

The few men who answered this question in the negative were all gay.

Even men that claimed to be happily married were able to relate to this frustration, and indeed many of those men attributed their "happy marriage" to the fact that they gave their wives whatever they wanted with no questions.

That's hypergamy in action, and it's a form of exercised power that is unequaled in its ability to control a man's life. It's all but universal to the male experience.

For men who desire the ability to avoid that trap, giving hypergamy an expanded definition is in order.

Hypergamy is the innate tendency in women to reduce men to mere utilitarian value, to extract as much value from men as possible and to continue to do so until the man's energy and resources are exhausted.

In short, hypergamy is the universal drive in women to turn men into appliances, and whether that appliance is a dildo or an ATM or both, makes little difference.

At this point, some female readers (and some men) will be screaming that not all women are like that. Sorry, but one way or another ALL heterosexual women practice hypergamy, and my money is on the idea that most lesbians do as well. It's biological programming, not a conscious choice. Hating women for it is about as useful as hating men for liking tits and ass.

And besides, one need not hate women to understand and counteract hypergamy. It's possible to force any woman into chasing her tail in circles, leaving her, karmically speaking, to experience the frustration that she usually is the one to inflict. And it does not require scheming, manipulation, dishonesty or any of the other less savory aspects of normal relationships.

In fact, it demands that you do just the opposite of those things and operate only in honest, direct ways that hinge on your self-respect and values.

Go back to the start of this piece and see the quote by Chris Rock. "Fuck your dreams, your ambitions and anything else that is important to you. It's all about her."

When you can encounter ideas like that, and your default response is "fuck that," you are well on your way to the healing. Just never forget that the onus is on you.

Dick Heart and the Crazy Cat Lady

I often write about spotting problems in women before they get a chance to piss in your Cheerios. I've done essays on the subtle and not so subtle indicators of borderline and other personality disorders. I have done pieces on deal breakers with women, which also include warning signs about what to look for.

All this boils down to one central idea. The warning signs of high-maintenance, fucked-in-the-head women are always there. ALWAYS. And I say this as a guy who has stepped on more than one relationship landmine without knowing I was in a minefield. Looking back, the signs were always there. Like screaming in my stupid face. I just wasn't listening.

My alter ego, a guy named Dick Heart, was always distracting me. And let me tell you, EF Hutton has nothing on Dick Heart. With a single word, he can make you not notice the smell of shit in an auction barn and he only shuts up after he gets you into trouble, which is pretty much any time you listen to him. Seriously, the warning signs of problem women are so numerous and obvious and common that I should not need to write about them and wouldn't were it not for Dick Heart.

The thing is that even if every problem woman in the world had a skull-and-crossbones tattooed across her forehead, the Dick Heart that lives in almost every man would refuse to see it. At least till she started ripping his life a new one, vaporizing his money and self-respect. That is when you find yourself standing there, scratching your head, asking how in tarnation did this happen?

Dick Heart, guys. He ain't your friend.

I mean, really, there are so many warning signs of problem women that you can break them down into categories, one of them being comedy. How crazy is that? And like always, I am not just laying the blame on women for this. Our culture creates so much bullshit in women that some of it is downright funny. And I don't mean some lame, feminized ghostbusters funny that isn't funny at all. I mean Bill Burr, Sam Kinison, Bill Hicks *laugh until you fucking cry* funny.

Let's look at some of the things that should A), make you laugh, and B), make you walk away with extreme prejudice.

One, she's 30 years old and her bed is covered, and I mean covered, with stuffed animals. Guys, when you see this shit, look for the ceramic unicorn on the side table. Keep nosing around her stuff and you will probably find a ton of other reminders that a huge piece of her life is still resisting puberty.

That one ties directly into another warning sign that should move you to run a hundred-meter dash in under 10 seconds in the opposite direction. She baby talks. I mean, seriously, have you ever had a woman talk to you like you were a fucking puppy? "Oh, sweetums, do you willy, willy wuv me?"

If you can hear that kind of talk without puking, you're a better man than me. If you like that kind of talk from a grown woman, please put down this book immediately. Come back and finish it when you reach puberty.

A grown woman baby-talking to a man she is having sex with is creepy. Imagine her, spread out on a pile of stuffed animals, wearing a teddy, baby-talking while she wiggles her finger at you to come to bed. You wanna let Freud take a shot at analyzing that scene?

Trust me, you don't. It's just too weird.

Speaking of weird, how about women who hoard cats? The standard, stereotypical crazy cat lady became the standard stereotypical crazy cat lady for a reason. First, I don't know about you, but it doesn't do much for me when the first thing you notice about a woman's home is that it reeks of cat shit. That one will even make Dick Heart do a double take. Seriously, give me a chain smoker any time. Or maybe a woman who has a meth lab in her basement. But the pungent smell of cat shit is the smell of crazy. It is *Eau de fucking loon*. Bet on it.

I was just discussing this with a female friend, an actual non-crazy human being, and we were questioning how many cats it took to qualify a woman for crazy. We seemed to hover around the question on whether three cats crossed the line or if it took more than three cats to qualify as crazy territory, but we did agree on one thing. Any more than one litter box comes with a woman primed to be pushing a shopping cart down the street, talking to herself with a streak of lipstick running up the side of her cheek.

Full disclosure here. I am not a big fan of cats to begin with, but I understand why some people like them. The thing is, when your pets come in herds, you are not taking care of them. They are taking care of something missing in you. We all have holes to fill in our lives, but if you meet a woman trying to fill hers with nine cats, do yourself a favor and keep on stepping.

By the way, just having one cat is not proof of sanity. I dated a woman once who told me that her cat had to approve of me. I thought she was joking till I figured out she really wasn't. We didn't have a chance. I decided to hate that cat before I ever met it.

Another comical giveaway on the road to feminine insanity is the selfie queen. And folks, if selfie queens were cats, the internet would be one great big litter box. There is nothing, and I mean nothing more revealing about a woman than a Facebook page crammed with self-snapped pictures of her pursing her lips with a stupid attempt at an "I'm so hot" look on her face.

There was a version of this that went on before the internet. When I first met my ex, she had a long table in her foyer that was sagging beneath the weight of framed pictures. Every one of them was her. There must have been 30 or 40 images of her in different poses on the one table. There was her, sitting in her car. Her on the sofa. Her in the studio with her chin resting lightly on her fingers, gazing upward toward some enlightened state. Her sitting at a table in a local café, smiling cutely over a cappuccino.

She had actually created an early 90's version of a millennial chick's Facebook page in her fucking foyer. Now, my actual brain should have looked at that with some concern about narcissism and self-obsession. Instead, Dick Heart looked at the picture of her on the beach and whispered, "nice tits" into my ear. I was off and running for the complete disaster.

The point here, gents, was that in case you didn't notice, the baby-talking, cat-herding, selfie-snapping woman with a stuffed animal zoo is out there in abundance. And she promises to reveal exactly who she is in the long run; a cauldron of craziness and terminal immaturity.

Getting a woman who talks in goo goo gaga vernacular when you meet her will absolutely start throwing tantrums to get her way before you manage to escape. She is, quite literally, a child. Think about that before you do anything stupid.

The same for Crazy Cat Lady. She is trying desperately to fill an empty hole in her life. She's trying so hard you can smell it on the other side of a closed door. It's only a matter of time before you become one of the cats.

Ditto for the selfie-queen. I mean, seriously, do I need to explain this? Just check out all of her selfies. Chances are she's wearing a t-shirt that says, "Proud Bitch," or "More Me, Less You." The writing may not be on the wall, but it is on her tits. If her tits are all you can see, don't be surprised when your life turns to shit.

Stuffed animals everywhere, unicorns on the wall, any and all other hallmarks of an immature mind will be present and visible in a woman's life; right out there in the open for you to see. Nobody's ever called her on it, so she doesn't see anything wrong with it.

And she's right. There's nothing wrong with staying a 10-year-old forever, provided you're careful to avoid screwing up the lives of grown men. But there's the problem. These terminal children disguised as women see grown men in one light only.

Daddy.

And not the disciplining adult daddy, but the big, strong daddums who will give widdle girl anything widdle girl wants. That's how big strong daddums ends up getting the life sucked out of him.

Dick Heart will tell you that pandering to women-girls is a good idea. But like I said, Dick Heart is not your friend. Dick Heart thinks he can kill you and keep going. The best thing to say to him when he starts whispering in your ear is, "Thank you for sharing. Now shut the fuck up."

Men & Women

The Real Reasons to Not Get Married

One of the central realities of the men's marriage strike is a reaction to the laws governing divorce. And it is an understandable position. Marriage, and subsequently divorce, puts men at some very serious risk. To name a few items that have been a relentless part of the anti-marriage drumbeat, we have the very real possibility of losing child custody and the authority of fatherhood (while still paying financially for the child), the loss of property and income that can accompany ruinous divorce settlements, and the loss of personal reputation that usually follows injudiciously dispensed restraining orders. Restraining orders and divorce, by the way, go together like Halloween and candy and are handed out with similar abandon. It is almost always men on the receiving end.

All this is not to mention the loss of liberty and life that can be the result of legal and social abuses that stem from marriage and divorce.

Feminists have insisted for decades that marriage is an institution that enslaves women and turns them into chattel that can cook and wash dishes. Of course, they're wrong, like every other time feminists open their mouths, but I suppose we should thank them, and maybe even support their cause if it makes women less inclined to marry.

Enough about feminists, though, and back to the topic at hand. Men's advocates have been documenting the legal hazards of marriage for a long time. You can find an abundance of that information online with very little effort. And since that work is so complete, I'd like to talk about some of the other reasons why it is better to avoid a hike toward the altar.

This is for the benefit of men who have somehow convinced themselves that they are insulated from the legal hazards. Perhaps they've convinced themselves that their darling "Cupcake" is their personal saint. She would never avail herself to the weapons provided by society and the state that are designed to destroy men (and their children) during the process of a divorce.

For these men I have a simple declaration. If the entirety of the corrupt family law system spontaneously, magically repaired itself; if restraining orders suddenly required proof; if alimony and child support were ended and equal and shared parenting became the law of the land, most men would still be better off unmarried and even not cohabitating, especially if their relationships were founded on any notion of romantic love.

So, for the sake of this discussion, let's toss out any and all concerns about what the law can do to a man and instead look at what long-term relationships do to men when romantic love and chivalry are integral to the foundation.

First, let's look at how most relationships begin. And let me be brutally honest about it even if most men won't be brutally honest with themselves. Relationships start with men competing to present themselves as capable protectors and providers for women. Straight out of the gate it is not about your character, your personality, or your decency as a human being. Nor is it about your capacity to love, communicate or be a good father.

It's not even about your looks or your sexual prowess. Those items count when women are looking for sex much more so than when women are looking for marriage. Which is to say that looks and stud qualities may well help her decide who she would cheat on you with, but not much else.

I don't care who you are, these are the ground rules that govern your involvement with women. I am not saying that there aren't unicorns out there who are exceptions. I am saying though, that they are unicorns, infinitesimally rare exceptions to the rule. And so far, we have not even factored in the neurotic expectation of entitlement that permeates western female culture.

Now, I'd like you to consider the average scene that you have witnessed your whole life with men proposing marriage to women. I don't need to fill in any imagery for you because in your mind's eye you can already see the man, kneeling on one knee, his hand lifting up an offering to the woman. Diamonds and gold, beckoning her acceptance.

Now picture yourself as the man in that scene. Waiting for word from that vision of joy standing above you, inspecting the ring. Waiting for her yes or no. Her thumbs up or thumbs down. Her acceptance of you forever, or her rejection of you that is just as permanent.

Can you see it? Good. Now understand one thing. You must get used to seeing yourself in that position, offering a lavish bribe in exchange for being "loved." You must get used to it because this is the defining moment of your future. This is the model for the entirety of married life.

Before you rush to convince yourself otherwise, I urge you to ask yourself one question. This vision, this age-old image of a man on his knees bearing jewels, holding his breath, waiting for her approval or ultimate rejection.

Do you think this is all happenstance? Perhaps an accident or some strange coincidence that doesn't really form a picture of married life?

Please read on.

What used to be something symbolic, a metaphor for the ability and willingness to be a provider, is now taken literally by legions of women. To them, this doesn't say, "I love you and want to marry you," it says, "I bring gifts because I owe you. Because your wants are more important than my needs." And her response isn't just, "Yes, I will marry you." It is, "You're goddamn right you owe me, and you will spend the rest of your life proving it."

If you don't believe that, then I can only ask you to take a look at the lives of so many married men who end up eternally yoked to lazy, self-absorbed harridans whose only real expertise in life is sloth, and haranguing their husbands into working ever harder to meet their childish desires.

They tend toward emotional, psychological and even physical abusiveness. Mind you, I'm not talking about abuse in the classic sense.

I am talking about the everyday, mundane type of abuse to which most men acclimate themselves.

Women getting their way about everything is one such form of abuse. It is the kind of abuse for which men frequently end up creating euphemisms. Like, "Oh, that's just how women are."

Well, yes. That is just how women are. The question is why are men so quick to put up with it? For instance, one of the things men will "get used to" in so-called successful marriages is that every major decision that impacts their lives is going to be made by her.

Any real estate agent will tell you that when a couple purchases a home, usually the most significant and costly decision of their lives, it is the woman who is going to make the decision. Even if you are the one paying the mortgage, agents know you probably don't count for much in the equation. They are selling to her, not you, or even you as part of a couple. They pitch the bitch. You're just the wallet.

This isn't limited to homes. According to Martha Barletta, author of *Marketing to Women*, US women control or influence 7 trillion dollars in consumer spending annually and make 85% of all purchase decisions. And note that the 85% is about *all* purchase decisions, not just the home. That means, at least statistically speaking, that the moment you get married, the lion's share of your purchasing decisions are no longer yours.

They're in *her* hands. She will decide on the car or cars you own, the furniture you buy, the vacations you take, even the clothing and food you shop for.

Ever heard of the stereotype of the couple in the mall, him carrying all the packages, two steps behind her as she forges ahead carrying nothing but the credit cards? Well, it's not an urban myth. Mall mules are real. And the most direct path to assuming that role is directly through matrimony.

And once you're there, the prospect of divorce takes on a whole new meaning.

Indeed, the more you examine the realities of marriage and divorce, the more apparent it becomes that divorce is just a demarcation line between her spending your money while you're still allowed to sleep in the home and spending your money after you've been kicked out.

Now consider that more than half of all marriages end in divorce.

OK, you might say, you're not really a materialistic guy and you don't mind if she spends your hard-earned cash in ways that please her. My experience is that this is the rationale of men whose spines resemble overdone strands of fettuccine and must rationalize their way out of looking at that, but I am not here to argue about it.

The fact is that it does not end with just turning you into a walking, talking ATM. In many cases, you are turned into an ATM that is not allowed to take up too much room in her house. Even when you technically live there.

After years of hearing from men who learned to cope with being viewed as a utility, who adjust to homes with hers and hers closets, hers and hers sinks, and hers and hers spending money, the disappearing personal space becomes just another thing they rationalize as some sort of noble sacrifice in the name of being a good man. This often persists as marriages become sexless and emotionally strangling.

So, men, as it turns out, must continue to rationalize through it all. As they watch their friends fade away, their interests and hobbies gather dust, and as they watch their whole lives reduced to an afterthought in the name of satisfying whatever it is she wants.

Just as they will have to put the rationalization hamster on steroids to conjure up a way to live with the fact that when all is said and done, *she will still be highly unlikely to approve of him.*

And there's the rub, gents. Life with modern women is nothing less than a battle for your soul. These days, women were born and raised in a culture that taught them that men owed them the moon and stars. They have been fed a narrative by feminists and traditionalists alike that tells them they are entitled. You have likely fed that narrative yourself at one time or another, assuming you're not doing it now.

Any woman you know, especially if she's attractive, has had men drooling over her, willing to endure any shame or sacrifice, just to be next to her. Even for a *chance* to be next to her.

So, when you hear some men talking about marriage as a trap, as a form of slavery, they are not just talking about what the state will do to you. Sadly, most men have been complicit in this modern tragedy.

This is one of the overarching challenges of marriage, and one of the universal dangers therein; losing yourself to the role of a matrimonial patsy for the sake of pleasing an eternally frustrated princess.

You may consider it a pittance to pay when you're 21, insecure and willing to pay anything for the illusion of love from the object of your desires. You may be willing to overlook the fact that even in your illusion there's no room for your self-respect.

You will see it very differently at 41, with two decades of your life wasted on someone who looks at you like a pack animal. Even then, it may be hard to look at yourself in the mirror and see that you did it to yourself.

I reiterate that there are a few unicorns out there. But of course, in the throes of infatuation and romantic love, every man thinks that is just what he has found. Nearly every one of them is wrong.

It's true that we need to revamp family law before marriage will ever be safe again. We also need to revamp women.

And, thankfully, with the growth of a new narrative, men are starting to revamp themselves.

Finally, allow me to regale you with a story once told to me by a psychiatrist I used to work with who happened to be Jewish.

He explained to me the difference between a schlemiel, a schlimazel and a schmuck. "Paul," he said. "Say there are three guys having dinner together. The Schlemiel is the guy who spills his soup. The Schlimazel is the guy who he spills it on. The schmuck is the guy who cleans it up."

So, in closing, let me say this. Please, don't be a schmuck. Don't get married. Not until some very big changes have happened in the world. In the meantime, do your part to make those changes happen, starting with what you see in the mirror.

Eight Laws Governing Men and Women

Italy, the United States, the Congo, the United Kingdom, South Korea, Denmark, Australia, Mexico, India, Japan, Canada and Spain. It is a very disparate (and only partial) list of countries, a blend of east and west; an extreme mix of languages and cultures spanning the entire planet. However differentiated in terms of societal norms and governance, however stark the surface contrast, all these places do have one very powerful and prominent thing that inextricably weaves through the fabric of their very existence, uniting them.

It is the same common thread that now runs through many other familiar entities: the Pentagon, Federal Express, the European Union, all conservative political parties, rock and roll music, the Prime Minister of the United Kingdom, nearly every criminal code on earth, the Australian Parliament, country music, all liberal political parties, all Fortune 500 companies, Oxford University, Fox News, the United Nations, The Salvation Army, the Ford Foundation and The New York Times.

What all these institutions, countries, cultures, corporations, and constructs have in common is that to a greater or lesser degree (usually greater), they have been impacted by the spread and influence of gender feminism.

We see it in the wholesale acceptance of manufactured research results and bogus statistics supporting the feminist narrative. These statistics are parroted without consideration or vetting by media outlets, state functionaries and political candidates (regardless of party) worldwide.

It is visible in the exponential rise in draconian laws that eviscerate canons of law that have stood for centuries; railroading innocent men into shackles and making them the property of a prison-industrial complex that has risen into prominence in the last 50 years.

It shows itself in college "honor courts" that have become star chambers, meting out life-altering consequences to young men without proof.

We are bombarded by it from the media, bombastically pounding us with disinformation and blackmailing us with the shame they have been instilling in us for decades.

We often joke, and with good reason, about the stupidity of feminists. After all, have you ever seen David Futrelle in a debate, watched Anita Sarkeesian damsel herself while complaining about damseling, listened to Jessica Valenti whine about being sexualized and not being sexualized in the same breath, or read a few lines of Ally Fogg just after he tells you he is not a feminist?

In fact, in the realm of feminism, particularly online, stupidity is regarded as good breeding; an asset that will get you to the top.

But the question remains, if feminists are so stupid, then why is feminism now a dominant ideology on the planet, affecting almost every institution, political apparatus, provider of every level of education, as well as every law enforcement agency and corporate entity known?

If feminists are so intellectually vacant, then why are we here, without resources and struggling mightily to skate by on guile and creativity in order to do anything about the supposed idiots?

The answer to that is as simple as it is forbidding.

Feminism is not for feminists. Feminists are idiots, but they are the useful idiots in the description previously reserved for Soviet sycophants in Cold War America.

Feminism is for governments and corporations. And it is the most effective tool for control of the masses since the riot baton and water cannons.

As we look across the map, from Stockholm to San Diego, from Tokyo to Toronto, we are not seeing a world that has just bought into the gender-dominated ramblings of a bunch of morons who could not cut it in STEM. Nor are we seeing the work of regressive female troglodytes sporting Doc Martins, one eyebrow and lip hair that aspires to be a moustache.

What we are seeing is a chain of governments, and just as importantly their powerhouse corporate interests, that have figured out the "secret" to inflicting whatever serves them on the populace without causing significant resistance.

They have found that the best method for making people toe the government line is not with iron-fisted restrictions on freedom of speech, the press or the right to assembly. Those are old world strategies still at play in some Third World regions, but not in the industrialized world. Sure, social media platforms are Orwellian in their propensity to silence dissent, but the government hasn't embraced that trend.

First World governments, and even some who barely qualify have discovered that they can control the masses with aggressive gynocentrism.

The method for doing so is not that difficult. All it takes is a little time, a little money, and more than a little basic understanding of human sociobiology. In fact, if you play your cards anything less than sloppy, you can control the masses with enthusiastic help - from the masses.

There are some basic laws that form the foundation for this kind of control. They are based on characteristics that trend heavily in the respective sexes. They are not 100% fixed, and there are exceptions, which of course means they are not laws in the scientific sense. The term law is used illustratively, not literally.

The exceptions are rare. There are very few of them comparatively; not enough to get in the way of asserting control if you are committed to it.

Discussing these laws requires some advance qualification. In them, you will see many blanket and highly generalized statements about men and women, much of it unflattering. Keep in mind two things. One, these laws deal with specific areas of sexually rooted behavior and attitudes. They are not intended as any kind of complete description of men and women. They are merely microcosms.

Second, the criticism is balanced. Not out of an orchestrated attempt to be egalitarian, but because the behaviors to be found here are of equal proportion in both men and women. I am not painting one as better, more moral or more principled than the other because that is not the case. When it comes to the human weaknesses that allow and enable this kind of tyranny, men and women find themselves in the rare position of being absolute equals.

So, let us begin.

The Eight Laws Governing Men and Women

Men:

1. Men will not oppose anything *perceived* to benefit women. Protecting women and providing for them and their children takes primacy over critical thinking. Note that the law says "perceived." It matters not if something benefits women, or if, in fact, it harms them. If the *perception* is popular that something benefits women, men will support it, even at their own expense and to their detriment.

2. Men will attack and shun other men for violating law number one. This relates to enforcement. The perception qualification still applies. In the social, legal and political realms, men will attack, verbally and physically, men who are perceived to either harm women or who oppose anything perceived to protect women. In fact, in the minds of men, those two things, harming women or opposing an attempt at their protection, are literally the same thing.

3. Men have almost no limits to how far they will go regarding adherence to laws number one and two. This includes the fact that men will have their own families ripped apart by corrupt courts. They will endure false allegations, alienation from their children, loss of home and income, staving off suicidal impulses, and ultimately react to it all by seeking another wife. They will tell other men who experience the same treatment that they need to shut up, or *man* up, and take it. They

will view a man who does not support VAWA as a man who supports domestic violence. They will view a man who does not support rape shield laws as a man who supports rape. The list goes on.

4. Men will not complain collectively about anything that happens to them. This crucial law is particularly beneficial to achieving complete governmental/corporate control. Attacks and affronts to men as a group will not cause a collective reaction. Ever. You can imprison men, beat them, steal their property, demonize their sons, psychologically destroy their children, relegate them to the streets, tax them and spend their money on other groups and as a group, they will not react. Again, ever. Indeed, men will, in accordance with laws number one and two, assist the state in the furtherance of such abuses provided the dominant public perception is that it is done in the name of protecting women.

Women:

1. Women will not oppose anything *perceived* to benefit them as a group. On the surface, this may seem innocuous and even just human, but it results in some decidedly inhuman outcomes. As a group, women will not oppose anything, no matter how destructive it may be to others, and ultimately themselves, if they perceive an immediate benefit. They won't, as a group, oppose all male Selective Service, all male genital mutilation or taking the lion's share of resources produced by men and redistributing them to women. They will not object to any other injustice that works in their favor. They will not oppose clearly oppressive and unconstitutional laws, provided they perceive a benefit to women. They will not oppose the complete disappearance of men from education and the workplace, provided they perceive it works to their advantage.

2. Women will attack and shun other women for violating law number one. The women who violate that law are frequently considered "traitors" to other women, and they will be marginalized and ostracized. The nature and scope of the attacks against them are generally less extreme than those against men, but they are completely real. Women will attack and shun other women for supporting any ideas that do not include women as the primary and often sole

beneficiaries of social services, special legal protections, government subsidies and even deference to opinions. Women, by and large, are women first and women only.

3. Women have virtually no limits to how far they will go regarding adherence to laws number one and two. This includes willingness to see their own children psychologically damaged for perceived personal advantage and seeing male loved ones abused and even destroyed by the state and other entities for the advantage of other women. They may experience outrage over how that abuse and destruction impacts them and the men they hold dear, but it will not translate into a meaningful outrage over what happens to men as a class.

4. Women will complain collectively about whatever happens to them as a group, regardless of whether it is really happening. The only requirement is that some level of perception of a problem is there. Women, as a group, will complain for decades about long debunked injustices against them and refuse to even entertain evidence to the contrary. Men will do this, too, but for women, not for themselves. The result of law number four is that it informs government and corporate entities that to pass laws and justify political policy, all it needs to do is frame information, accurate or not, in a way that paints women as a victim class. Sociobiology will take over from there.

These are the laws on which modern tyranny is built. Why? Because these laws determine what people will vote for and what they will tolerate. Again, they are not presented to pass moral judgment on men or women. These traits are an innate part of the human condition in both sexes. Faulting women as a class for blindly taking advantage of unfair laws is only as legitimate as faulting men for enabling and abetting the exact same thing.

These laws are passed with the support of both sexes. Failing to recognize that also blinds us to the possible solutions, whatever they may be.

What is important here is to take this understanding of the predictability of attitudes and behavior innate in men and women, and see how those things might be exploited to exert control over the masses; to intrude unreasonably into private life, which might just be a clue as to how it has already happened.

What would we do if we wanted a government and/or a corporate hegemony that could work unimpeded toward any end it wanted, and without the nuisance of legal or civil rights concerns getting in the way?

A good place to start is to disempower the average man (not the .01% at the top). Make the average man a default criminal, not even fit to sit next to a child on a plane. Turn him into a looming, potential threat who demands management. Treat him as a potential rapist and an abuser. Tie it all to the protection and advantage of women.

Done.

Set up law enforcement and legal entities that are geared primarily to interdict on masculinity itself, or rather the version of masculinity being sold by those in charge. Use it mercilessly. Throw due process and presumed innocence out the window. Make it socially unpopular to even object to it. This works especially well in minority communities that will complain vociferously about racial profiling but will fall silent when the discrimination is based on sex and is against men. Count on the silence and enforcement for non-compliance guaranteed by the laws that govern men and women to be in overdrive here.

Check that one off the list, too.

Men are much more likely to challenge authority, e.g. their own governments, when the well-being of their families are at stake. It is therefore essential to strip away male authority and presence in the family. Make divorce easily accessible, even popular, profitable, and stack the deck against men in family courts. The laws of men and women will ensure they stay largely silent about it, no matter how bad it gets, no matter how much harm it causes, even as it destroys children. And it won't matter in the long run, those children will grow into consumers, too. Money from damaged people spends just as well.

Some of them will grow into criminals because of these abuses, but they can be incarcerated. That too is a business.

Tick the box on this one, also.

Remove men from higher education and any part of the workforce in which being a man is not essential. Keep men in ditches, trucks, fishing boats and the unemployment line. Make them as unattractive as possible for selection in starting families. Use them to wage war when corporate interests are at stake, and if they are married, assist the wives in finishing them off once they return from the front, broken or deemed dangerous. They won't complain. They may kill themselves, but they won't complain. Women won't complain, either. In fact, both will feel good about it, or at least act like they do. It is in the sociobiology. Remember the laws.

This one is in progress. Outlook promising.

Systematically indoctrinate women into the mindset that they are victims. Feed them disinformation until they feel they are owed the right to inflict whatever harm they want on the deemed criminal class and provide the state services needed to assist them. A fabricated wage gap becomes a gender gap. An imaginary glass ceiling becomes a very real glass wall in almost no time. A status as a sole victim in domestic disputes becomes a license to physically attack men and then call state functionaries to haul off your victim.

Double check.

Give women a false sense of empowerment.

It is easiest to do this as you make a public display of the disempowerment of men. They will see it happening in front of their eyes and then swear it is a man's world because on some level they know that crazy belief is fueling the actual disempowerment they are witnessing.

Shame women for valuing motherhood more than professional life. Help them view their children and especially their husbands as hindrances rather than assets. Socialize them to value work and the state over motherhood and family. Push them toward low paying (but taxable) jobs, while binding them to state-provided subsidies like WIC, food stamps, welfare, child support and alimony. Make them obedient taxpaying consumers that support feminist governance because for many of them it will be the difference between just being poor and being really impoverished. Make them financially and psychologically dependent on their own enslavement.

Tell them they can achieve the top, then point them toward the middle and lock them in. Do all this and put a gun in their hand that they can use on men at will, and they will be obedient servants of the state for life. Remember, if they *perceive* they have the advantage, that they are empowered, even sitting there in a corporate cubicle, missing their child with dark bags under their eyes, they will act like puppets on a string.

Done, done and done.

The point here is that feminism is not a sweeping movement for change or a way to liberate women (and allegedly men) from the burdens of their sexual role in the world. It is not a movement for equality or justice.

Feminism is nothing more than a government tool by which governments can roughly double the number of taxpayers; by which civil liberties can be swept aside so that money can be extracted. It is a way to eviscerate freedoms on every level while getting the population to do the bulk of the work to make it happen. *It is a way to insert government control into every possible aspect of modern human life, from the bedroom to the boardroom.* It is not stupid. It is fucking brilliant in an evil sort of way.

The true order of things is hidden behind the façade created by the eight laws, where governments and corporations are increasingly taking over our lives and our minds. Feminists are not a bunch of nut cases that have taken over the world. They are just a bunch of nut cases that have assisted some smart and devious people in erasing any impediments they might have ever had at putting a leash on all of us.

And now comes the Red Pill Revolution. That would be us. We are a tiny but growing minority, even as the zombies living by the eight laws are showing some signs of shrinkage. At the very least they are finally getting exposed to a couple of things they don't much like.

The truth, and public humiliation.

I'd call that a good place to start.

Men, Math and Marriage

I've been sitting here for the last 30 minutes, fingers poised over my laptop, frozen. Rather they have a slight tremble, like all the keys are painted with cyanide and my fingers know it.

I've decided to do a piece offering some marital advice to men. And I know men well. I might as well be doing a porn review for the readers of Ms. magazine. But I am feeling dangerous and my fingers are starting to work, so here goes.

My first piece of advice for men when it comes to marriage is simple.

Don't. And I do mean never. And, yes, that means you.

I don't cotton much to psychobabble, so I won't make a hypocrite of myself by making you endure any of it from me. Thankfully, psychobabble is not necessary. For it isn't relationship dynamics that will get you. It's math. And the numbers are scary.

First, and most of you know this, more than half of all marriages end in divorce, not counting the ones that end in murder, suicide and psychiatric facilities. But that doesn't mean that only half of marriages are failures. There are a lot of failed marriages that don't end in divorce. These are people who stay married and make a hobby of hating each other like Democrats and Trump supporters.

And the math on marriage isn't near as disturbing as the numbers you will face when it's over. The equation goes roughly something like this.

1 angry wife + 1 lawyer + 1 family court = 1 impoverished man living in a studio apartment and driving a 1995 Buick.

Numbers are sometimes ugly, but they don't lie.

But wait, you say, I can change that equation with a prenup!

Yes, you can. Here are the factor-weighed results.

1 angry wife + 1 lawyer + 1 family court + 1 prenuptial agreement = 1 impoverished man living in a studio apartment and driving a 1996 Buick.

Prenups take more time to draw up than the courts take tossing them aside.

The fact of the matter is that in modern society men are better off downing ten shots of tequila and walking blindfolded through a minefield than to get married. Minefield odds are better.

Think about it for a moment. Marriage is quite literally an investment of not only your heart but of all your work, income and future income, especially when children are involved. Now, if an investment broker told you he had a deal in which you could invest, and there was more than a 50% chance that you would be wiped out and spend most of your life paying the margin call or going to jail, how much would you invest?

Well?

Oh, come on now, you might be saying. It's not fair to reduce the institution of marriage into a financial equation. Well, yes, it is. Believe me, if the woman you marry doesn't heavily consider your income prior to saying yes, she is the infinitesimal exception. And for those of you who still think it is natural and right for a man to be the breadwinner and the head of the family, please know that would be the same head that gets lobbed off in the family court where more than half of you will end up.

And even if you don't think, for who knows what reason, that marriage isn't in large part a financial arrangement, you can bet your ass that divorce is. Reducing holy matrimony to assets and liabilities is precisely what family courts are designed to do. And they do it with brutal efficiency. If you walk into one of those places expecting justice and fairness, you will find out how naïve you are in the most sobering ways imaginable.

A lot of married men already know this. Those are the guys in the other half of the marriage statistics. You know, the group that is "successful?" Plenty of them have consulted lawyers because they wanted to escape insufferably nasty, horrifically high-maintenance wives, but the more legal realities they heard, the more those banshees to which they were married regained their appeal. As soon as they coined the phrase "take him to the cleaners," the follow-up, "cheaper to keep her," wasn't far behind.

Just don't do it.

Living with a woman may be a better option, but you need to be careful with that one, too. Depending on the statutes where you live, you could end up married without knowing it. So, gather your facts.

Yes guys, that means go see a lawyer, one that understands men's legal issues, before you even shack up. Do it the moment she asks if she can leave some clothes in your closet. Better yet, do it now, while you don't have a girlfriend and can still think from the neck up. Consider the legal consult the investment of a lifetime, because it is.

And having children? Sure. Just be prepared for the very real possibility that every connection to those children will be severed when it's over. Except, of course, for the financial connection. That will be maintained at gunpoint.

So, choose that Buick carefully. You'll be driving it for a long time.

I know that some of you are thinking, "Oh, that will never happen to me." All I can say is that more than half of you are deluding yourselves, and the rest of you have no reliable way to know just how lucky you will be. For those who maintain that adolescent sense of invulnerability, such admonitions will fall on deaf ears. Never underestimate the power of denial.

I also know that some of you, especially some women that are reading this, are saying "Hey, wait! Not all women are like that! They are not all the same!" And you are right, they're not. But all family courts are the same. Screwed in L.A. Shafted in New York. Swindled in London. They are all the same.

Just don't do it.

Since you are likely not going to listen to me and make your own decisions, and you insist on taking that plunge, I have some suggestions on finding a suitable bride that might help with damage control down the road.

First, never finance a relationship. Only date women who pay their own way from the start. It will reduce your chances of dating and ultimately marrying women who will feel entitled to all your assets when and if it ends.

It leaves you with a better, if less common, class of woman. For if a woman feels that she is entitled to ride your wallet though life when she is infatuated with you, when you can do no wrong and are the most amazing man she ever met, just imagine how she will feel about your wallet when she hates the very sight of you and the sound of your voice makes her want to claw her own eyes out.

Watch her behavior and learn from it. How does she act when you disappoint her? What is her reaction to hearing the word "no," or when you choose your way instead of her way?

If she takes it in stride and moves on, then you might have a keeper, inflection on the word *might*.

However, if she responds to the fact that you went golfing when she didn't want you to by cutting you off in the bedroom for a few days, or by telling you how selfish and immature you are for having any interests that don't revolve around her, what do you imagine she will do when she fully believes that you are the Antichrist and are responsible for every ill in her miserable life?

And that, gentlemen, is precisely the woman you will face in a divorce. She won't be rational or reasonable or even principled. She will be, quite literally, your mortal enemy. And she will have the full force of the state on her side, ready to inflict retribution on you for her broken dreams, all of which will be your fault.

Make that a 1989 Buick.

And so, there you have it, guys. A blunt but nonetheless honest assessment of the modern state of matrimony which has become the legal equivalent of a slot machine. If you have been alive more than about an hour, you know someone to which the worst has already happened. Quite likely you know more than one. No one will fault you for pursuing the same goals that men have been pursuing for ages; wife, children, family and all that comes with it.

But we live in an age unlike any other in our history. All it takes to see that is the ability to do subtraction, hopefully before the state does it for you.

Just don't do it.

Women, Wallets and Waste

If all you want is periodic sex and companionship with a woman, then smile big. You owe that to yourself. Well, unless you are using your wallet to get there.

If that is the case, you are throwing away good money and putting yourself in the role of a John. If that floats your boat, more power to you. But you might want to keep reading anyway.

We will start with some uncomfortable basics.

Inconvenient fact #1

Women decide in the first five minutes (or seconds) of meeting you whether they want to bed down with you.

That is a fact that I will wager 90+% of men never get through their skulls.

Those five minutes, or seconds, are your only chance for influence over which way she goes with her decision, and your biggest hope for her deciding your way is not to give a damn what she decides.

I don't create the rules. I just observe them.

That is not to say that money can't play a role. A guy decked out in Armani and Italian leather will rise above others. All other things being equal, he will attract more women. He will also attract the very kind of woman who wants to take all that shit away from him the second she can get her claws in.

Inconvenient fact #2

Some guys get laid a lot more often. Whether it is money, movie star looks, a porn star cock and the skills to back it or a very serious (often innate) understanding of female psychology, some men just have an edge. Adjust your expectations accordingly. It is much easier to do that when you learn to aggressively manage that pathetic pining to get laid.

Ironically, learning to not be pathetic about women is one of the few things you can do to increase your sexual opportunities.

So even if more sex is your motive, the path to get there is a daily dose of Fuckitol™.

Inconvenient fact #3

Leading your dating life with your wallet is better described as paying a string of prostitutes in the hopes that one of them will deliver service.

Talk about hapless. This one takes the cake. Take an honest prostitute. She will go away when you are done and won't tell you that she doesn't like your shirt or that your friends drink too much. And more importantly, when you pay a hooker for sex, sex is what you get. Not a line about "let's be friends" or a request to get to know you better, which usually translates to "buy me some more dinners before I tell you we can 'just be friends.'"

Thankfully, there are also some decidedly *convenient* facts. Remembering them can help you think of your wallet as something other than where your money makes a quick pitstop before departing in a cloud of smoke.

Convenient fact #1

There are women who don't mind paying their own way. Sure, they are not falling out of trees. They are out there, though. And you can encounter them if you are the kind of man uninterested in any other kind of woman.

That means projecting your values to the people who know you, without compromise (and without a lot of fanfare).

You can even advertise in your social circles that you only do the 'Dutch thing'; that if you were a multi-millionaire you would not pay a woman to spend time with you. Feel free to let people quietly know that if you wanted an escort service, you have the internet.

If you don't make too much of a production of it; if you are not too ostentatious (and if you don't have leprosy or body odor) that will likely result in a woman expressing interest in you who may not have otherwise done so.

It will also turn off every goldbricking skeezer in the group. If you have been chasing tail with your wallet, you know just the kind of woman I am talking about. She already has some of your cash. Maybe a lot of it.

Convenient fact #2

Looks depreciate. Money appreciates. Two realities of life are at play here. Looking at them honestly can be a little chilling. One, a woman's looks depreciate with time. I am not just talking about time in the sense of crow's feet and sagging boobs. I am talking about the basic reality that you could be with the most beautiful woman in the world, a wild, incredible lover, and over a period of time, she would lose her luster.

Well, in your eyes anyway. It is no different for her. Man or woman, you have sex with the same person enough times and the passion fades. There may be some exceptions, but I am wagering not many.

The longer men and women stay together, the less emphasis and value they put on sex.

On the other hand, your money (aside from inflation) will be just as good in five years as it is right now. And if you're smart enough to have your money working for you, it will be worth more.

When you chase a woman with your wallet, her looks and your money both dry up on you. So put your freaking wallet up and just open your mind to a woman who fits your lifestyle. You will be in much better shape if and when it is over.

Convenient fact #3

You're in charge of all of this. You can either see yourself as someone just playing the cards they were dealt, or you can become the dealer.

You can live with the reality that money attracts whores, or you can enjoy the delusion that if you spend enough you will be wanted and loved.

Or, should you decide to take a different path, you can become hooker kryptonite and learn to better attract lower maintenance women, regardless of how much time you want to spend with them.

Château Bullshit

O.K., so you want to get laid? Here's how you do it. *Smell clean, put on some nice clothes, get in the proximity of women, and then ignore them.* When they come to fuck you, and they will, shut up and let it happen.

Sorry, but there is little else to it. Women are wired to respond to men who walk with enough self-confidence and involvement in their own lives that they don't need to invest any energy into bagging girls. They attract women naturally.

There now, I just told you in 85 words (and could have cut it to 50) everything anyone ever needed to know about scoring.

Unfortunately, the great majority of men have a really difficult time getting this, largely because they don't have any real confidence to project. It's been sucked out of them by this gynocentric world and it shows at its most glaring every time they get in the presence of women. The big problem here is that the pussy-attracting magic of indifference can only be feigned convincingly by a minority of men, which is why we have PUA's (pickup artists) out there in abundance teaching men how to jump through hoops trying to get women's attention and move in for the score (read: pussy begging).

It's a tad ironic, isn't it, that in a culture where women are more sexually aggressive and available than ever that we have men out there actually selling the idea that getting laid requires an artform?

What bullshit.

Don't get me wrong. I don't have anything against the high profile PUA's and the like. I also have a healthy respect for people who can sell designer lint removers with fossilized whalebone handles for $200 when a patch of masking tape and some common sense will work just as well. But it *must* be said that all these salespeople are targeting a similar demographic; ignorant, gullible customers. And in the case of PUAs they are exploiting the loneliness and isolation of mostly young men who suffered a lack of male role models, and therefore a lack of confidence. I must admit that making a living at that could be called an art, and probably should. It's a special kind of art. It's called con artistry.

I think in a way those guys do us a lot of good, though I wish I could say the same for their followers. The men's rights movement, something at which they sometimes like to take pot shots (it's that wannabe alpha dog thing), benefits from their work. I look at it this way. Red Pill life, the grownup version, is where a lot of PUA's end up once they get some whiskers and disabuse themselves of the misguided notion that getting laid is something you need to work at. Overcoming their denial can be tricky, though. The conversation usually goes something like this.

MRA: Man, you don't need to do all that work to get laid.

PUA: But hell man, I get PUSSY! And I feel so great about myself! Can't you tell?

MRA: I heard you. I am just saying that there are ways to get there that don't require work on your part, and they leave you feeling good enough that you don't need to try to sell anyone on how good you feel.

PUA: What are you talking about? Man, I get PUSSY! I feel great! I am awesome!

MRA: Well, bless your heart that's wonderful, but what I meant to say was that you don't need to do all that chasing. More gynocentrism isn't a healthy answer in a gynocentric world.

PUA: The more I chase, the more PUSSY I get! Wanna see my cold approach?!

MRA: Uh, no thanks. Don't you think a one-track mind on sex can be dangerous? I mean, given the times?

PUA: Man, you're never going to get any PUSSY talking like that!

Not much to work with, is it? And I am not really suggesting that anyone try. The men who end up being Red Pilled after being introduced to the Manosphere via PUA sites don't need to be fished out of the cesspool. They tend to walk out of it on their own, as would anyone who would not be Gamed by Gamers forever.

But the ones that remain, and make it a lifestyle, are just too enslaved to imagine Red Pill freedom, and likely not bright enough to learn what it means. They are literally institutionalized by their own desires and cannot imagine setting foot outside the city limits of Snatchville. The unquestionable black hole that exists in all these men is the place that should have held their core values and self-respect. And I must say after interacting with a few of them, their core values and self-respect, along with their integrity, are lacking.

Anyone who attempts to make an art form of passing a shit test has only succeeded in eating said shit and advertising themselves to the world as a shit eater (Yes, I know, but you get PUSSY!). Too bad such unfortunates seem oblivious to the fact that refusing to even participate in a shit test will have the same effect as passing one, except that it might help to eventually hook you up with a woman slightly less likely to yell rape the first time she gets pissed at you or cuts off your dick when you're asleep.

And anyone who believes in tossing negs, concocted for the purpose of aiding in the score, only does so because they don't realize that living by values that you don't retreat from, one of them being that your self-respect is worth more than borrowed time in a vagina, is the best neg you could ever hope to toss. But hey, if you like begging, eating shit and life with no values, The Château has room for you.

Some Gentle Thoughts on Marriage Counseling

While this book assumes a postmarital world, I also understand that some of you good gents have been married since before the worm turned and you started eating Red Pills. And some of you, a dwindling number, got married recently. All of you are welcome. This material is for you, too. Some of it specifically for you.

After all, you're a married man. But now you've realized that the honeymoon is over. Where once she whispered sweetly in your ear, she now nags incessantly. The curtain has closed on days filled with laughter, closeness, and hot sex, and they've been replaced by seemingly unending rounds of her zeroing in on every fault you have, real or imagined. She is chronically unhappy, and she's making sure she does not suffer that state alone.

You can see clearly that she has abundant reasons to enjoy life and that her dissatisfactions and frustrations are self-chosen but getting her to see that is like trying to scratch through granite with your fingernails. It's just not happening.

You used to look forward to seeing her after a day's work, but now the time you spend with her is just more work. You are wondering how your relationship turned into a second job, one that you like even less than your first job. And you are not getting any answers.

Your weekends, which you used to enjoy, are now emotional marathons. You pray for overtime and find more and more excuses to leave the house alone. Your conflicts (which were rare) used to be solved with relative ease. They have now become dead ends, bitter rounds of going nowhere. Every time you try to solve a problem it ends up feeling like you are circling the drain because she seems incapable of a single rational thought. Any expectations you have of her maturity and accountability are perceived as personal attacks.

And then, one day, she hits you with it. It may come at the end of a heated argument. Or perhaps during a quiet moment when you hear her utter the words "we need to talk" or something like that. Only you know that "we need to talk" doesn't mean both of you. It means *she* needs to talk, and she needs *you* to listen. To her, it just feels better to make it sound like she wants an actual conversation.

So, you roll your eyes or fidget in your chair, or quietly swear to yourself or do whatever it is you do when you see the freight train of her disapproval barreling down on you. You know it's coming, so you might as well say it, and you do. You hear yourself mumble "OK," resigned to the inevitable. You brace yourself for the impact.

This time, though, it's different. She opts out of her standard complaints *du jour* about what you didn't do that she clearly asked you to do, or what you did do that she asked you not to, or how much time you spend on videos, or friends, or work, or some other shit that does not revolve around her. She tells you instead that she is concerned about your relationship; your future together. She wants the problems that the two of you are having to find a solution. She wants whatever it is that is plaguing both of you to be solved. She says she wants you both to see a marriage counselor.

O.K. guys, I really want you to listen up here. No seriously, c'mere, a little closer. I want to make sure you hear this.

There now. Are you listening? I mean closely. You are? Good.

Don't fucking do it! For the love of everything holy, don't fucking do it!

You are better off going to the airport and screaming Allahu fucking Akbar at the TSA agents. Jail sucks and the cops might even put a pounding on you, but it's nothing compared to the ass-kicking you are going to get if you are dumb enough to go with her to a marriage counselor.

First, let's get a couple of points straight from the beginning. One, she is not trying to find solutions to your relationship problems. Well, in her mind she is because in her mind, *you're* the problem. If she can get *you* fixed, then *her* problems will be solved. She has no idea at all that she is, in fact, the source of a lot of the relationship's problems. She sees fixing you as a solution almost instinctively. She's been brainwashed her whole life into believing that all relationship problems are caused by men.

In a way, she's not that far from wrong. The deck is stacked in women's favor in marriage counseling and they know it. After all, it is marriage counseling types that have orchestrated a good bit of the brainwashing.

At some point in her life, she's read their books or watched them on TV or taken in their material on the internet – all of it focused on the wrongness of men. She just knows that if she can corral you into a marriage counselor's office, it'll be tag team on you. And she is 100% right. Don't delude yourself otherwise.

And there is something else you should know. Chances are that if you go with her into a marriage counselor's office, your problems will have puppies. Several litters.

Look, get this and get it good. Traditional therapy, especially marriage counseling, is a female-dominated *consumer product*. It is designed by women, for women. Family therapists don't try to sell their wares to men for the same reason that Snap-on doesn't try to sell their tools to women. There's no male market for marriage counselors. It's the wrong demographic. Their money is made from women, even if most of the money is ultimately coming from men. Marriage therapy is where women play and men pay, in more ways than one.

Marriage therapists know the rules as well as real estate agents. If you don't please the woman, you can kiss your business goodbye. Kinda resembles most marriages in that way. If you think marriage counselors rise above that to provide unbiased professional services, please slap yourself in the face as hard as you can and tell yourself to wake up.

Remember, the core of modern psychological training is ideological. That includes academicians who are steeped in profoundly retarded ideas like male privilege, patriarchy and other made-up non-realities they are pulling out of their asses these days. The psychological establishment has become one big, fat Gillette commercial. And they want to give you a clean shave.

Even if they weren't avaricious blowhards with advanced degrees in conjecture, they come from a standard of indoctrination that informs them you've been freaking wrong since the moment you were born with a penis. They firmly believe that you have power and privilege packed in your scrotum and that solutions for bad marriages start with pulling the rug out from underneath your feet. There will never be a way in their sessions to address the facts that you aren't privileged and that she isn't a victim.

Oh, and discussing the things she does to undermine the relationship? Forget about it. Push for it and the tag team will paint you as an abuser.

In other words, gents, if you are married to an insufferable, insatiable bitch who wants to go into counseling, and you agree, you will find yourself sitting in front of *two* insufferable, insatiable bitches who will identify you as broken and in need of repair. That is, after you genuflect to them both. It won't even matter if the second bitch is a man. The outcome will be the same.

Just like every other area of life, there are unicorns. I am sure there are marriage and family therapists with a balanced, non-ideological approach who don't see counseling couples as a sacrificial altar on which men are dispatched. I am sure there are unbiased, competent and even-handed practioners. If I ever meet one, I'll write a book about it.

Oh, on the outside chance that you like stepping on nails, sifting through hot coals with your bare fingers or stabbing yourself in the eye with a pencil, and you *still* want to give marriage counseling a shot, you will need some help trying to find that rare breed of therapist.

Here's what you do. Google *Licensed Marriage and Family Therapist* for whatever city you are in. Print out all 150 pages of returns and tape them up to a wall. Now, stand with your back to that wall on one foot and throw a dart with points on each end backward over your shoulder. If you are right-handed, use your left hand and vice versa. Then hop backward on one foot till the end of the dart sticks in your back. That part isn't necessary to pick your therapist. I just wanted you to get familiar with something sharp sticking in your back. You'll need the experience.

Finally, turn around and see the therapist the dart landed on. There's your huckleberry.

Doing things this way is as good as doing them any other. Seriously guys. If you have problems in your marriage, the best thing you can do is indulge in some self-care. You might ask yourself why you are willing to live with all this misery to begin with.

Seriously, do you want a relationship with Ms. Crazypants? Did you sign up for a life of unending criticism, her live streaming every one of your faults, real or imagined? Are you prepared for a lifetime of nagging and berating?

If the answer to any of those questions is yes, you don't need a marriage counselor, you need a psychiatrist and a swift kick in the ass.

The only shot you have at restoring balance to your relationship is to quit taking shit. Your only hope is to reconnect to your values, to your boundaries, and live what you believe. It's likely that your values don't include making allowances for abusive harridans.

The key is whether you're willing to see the harridan walk out for good. If you're not, you're fucked. If you are, you can't lose. It's just that simple. She will either change or leave if your values and your willingness to live by them is intact.

No marriage counselor needed or wanted.

Chasing the Dragon

Co-written with Peter Wright

Many students of sexual politics posit the "scientific" notion that our culture of gynocentrism is a basic biological reality; that we should either get with the program and enjoy it or bow out in a nihilistic fashion.

An alternative explanation of gynocentrism suggests it is merely an exaggeration of human potential; one that leads to social and reproductive failure despite common beliefs.

The bioscience lexicon can clarify this.

A *superstimulus* refers to the exaggeration of a normal stimulus to which there is an existing biological tendency to respond. An exaggerated response, or, if you will, a *superresponse*, can be elicited by any number of superstimuli.

For example, when it comes to female birds, they will prefer to incubate larger, artificial eggs over their own natural ones. Large, colorful eggs are a superstimulus. Leaving real eggs out to die is the superresponse.

Similarly, humans are easily exploited by junk food merchandisers. Humans are easily trained to choose products that cause heart disease, diabetes and cancer over the nutritious food they evolved to eat and thrive on, simply by playing tricks on the taste buds and manipulating the starvation reflex.

Sugar and refined carbohydrates are superstimuli. Consuming toxic food over healthy food is the superresponse.

The idea is that healthy human behavior evolved in response to normal stimuli in our ancestor's natural environment. That includes our reproductive instincts. The same behavioral responses have now been hijacked by the supernormal stimulus.

From this perspective, we see that a superstimulus acts like a potent drug, one every bit comparable to heroin or cocaine. Those drugs imitate weaker chemicals like dopamine, oxytocin, and endorphins, all of which occur naturally in our bodies.

As with drug addictions, the effects of *superstimuli* account for a range of obsessions and failures plaguing modern man – from the epidemic of obesity and obsessions with territoriality to the destructive, violent and suicidal behaviors central to our modern cult of romantic love.

An interesting tidbit about superstimuli of manufactured narcotics is the phenomenon known as "chasing the dragon." It is a term that originated in the opium dens of China, and it refers to what happens the first time a person inhales opium vapor. The resulting euphoria is complete, even magical - the first time.

Subsequent to that, the user tries again and again, with ever-increasing amounts of the drug, to re-create that first blissful high. They can't do it. The brain is now familiar with the flood of manufactured opiates. The user gets high and very addicted, but the magic of the first experience is an elusive butterfly.

They pursue it, though, with all their might, chasing the dragon they rode in their first experience.

We see a similar phenomenon with men trying desperately in their relationships with women to be rewarded with redeeming love, sex and approval, using Romantic Chivalry. It sends them, like an addict, traveling the path of a Mobius strip, going in circles, chasing the dragon.

There is little doubt how this happens.

Here are three examples of human superstimuli, and how they are used to elicit a destructive superresponse in the human male.

1. Artificially manufactured neoteny

Neoteny is the retention of juvenile characteristics in body, voice or facial features. In humans, neoteny activates what is known as the parental brain, or the state of brain activity that promotes nurturance and caretaking. The activation occurs through something called an innate releasing mechanism.

A classic example of an innate releasing mechanism is when seagull chicks peck at the parent's beak to get food.

Each adult seagull has a red spot on the underside of their beak, the sight of which instinctively triggers, or releases, the chicks to peck. It is the *innate releasing mechanism.*

This innate releasing mechanism, of course, is essential to the survival of seagulls, and there is something like it to be found in all birds and mammals — any creature that cares for its offspring. In mammals, juvenility is one of the innate releasing mechanisms that unconsciously determine our motivations to protect and provide, thus ensuring the survival of the species.

Juvenile characteristics in humans, however, can also be manipulated to garner attention and support that far exceeds the demands of survival.

In particular, neoteny is exploited by women to gain various advantages, a fact not lost on medical doctor and author Esther Vilar, who writes:

"Woman's greatest ideal is a life without work or responsibility – yet who leads such a life but a child? A child with appealing eyes, a funny little body with dimples and sweet layers of baby fat and clear, taut skin – that darling miniature of an adult. It is a child that woman imitates – its easy laugh, its helplessness, its need for protection. A child must be cared for; it cannot look after itself. And what species does not, by instinct, look after its offspring? It must – or the species will die out.

With the aid of skillfully applied cosmetics, designed to preserve that precious baby look; with the aid of helpless exclamations such as 'Ooh' and 'Ah' to denote astonishment, surprise, and admiration; with inane little bursts of conversation, women have preserved this 'baby look' for as long as possible so as to make the world continue to believe in the darling, sweet little girl she once was, and she relies on the protective instinct in man to make him take care of her."

Zoologist **Konrad Lorenz** discovered that images releasing parental reactions across a wide range of mammalian species were rounded heads and large eyes, compared with angular heads with proportionally smaller eyes that do not elicit such responses.

Lorenz compared those images with images of skillfully applied eye makeup by the modern woman in search of romance. The many-colored eyeshadows, eyeliners, and mascaras, not to mention the hours practiced in front of the mirror opening those eyes as wide as possible and fluttering – all designed to spur the viewer's paleo reflexes into action.

Neotenic female faces (large eyes, greater distance between eyes, and small noses) are found to be more attractive to men while less neotenic female faces are considered the least attractive, regardless of the females' actual age. And of these features, large eyes are the most effective of the neotenic cues – a success formula utilized from Anime to Disney characters in which the eyes of adult women have been supersized and faces rendered childish.

2. Exaggeration of sexual qualities

Clothing and postures which exaggerate the hips, thighs and breasts have been cultivated for millennia.

The cut, color, and drape of clothing; the underwear, corsets, lingerie and the shoes, hats, jewelry and other accessories make for a long study in the evolution of fashion – and in terms of sexuality they stand for nothing less than superstimuli designed to elicit an overload of sexual attraction in the viewer.

Perhaps more interesting on the enhancement front is the arrival of plastic surgery designed to transform the body into a theater of superstimuli, sometimes with grotesque, even fatal results. Such is the risk invited and embraced in the pursuit of enhanced sex-appeal.

Breast implants, butt implants, Botox injections, nose jobs, tummy tucks, facelifts – all designed for enhanced sexuality, and even more importantly, enhanced power and control.

3. Artificially intensified pair-bonding drive

We have all heard the advice of the seasoned matron to younger women; "Don't turn your love on like a tap or he will lose interest – withhold some affection and you'll always have him begging for more."

This message is now so widespread that animal-training techniques are being redeployed by women who wish to control their man's attachment needs.

In "How to Make Your Man Behave in 21 Days or Less Using the Secrets of Professional Dog Trainers," we read, "Consistently a dog is 'nicest' when he wants to be fed. Then he becomes all wags and licks. A known trick for keeping a dog on his best behavior is to just fill his bowl halfway so he's yearning for more.

Same goes for his appetite for affection. Keep him in constant emotional hunger for you and he'll be more attentive and easier to control."

As cruel as it sounds, withholding affection, sex, approval and love have become part of women's repertoire of superstimuli used to coerce men into service. Perhaps there was a time when that service could have been considered an appropriate response to a survival-oriented stimulus. Now, however, it has been replaced by superstimuli and male service has degenerated into a destructive superresponse.

Such dating advice for women abounds on the internet with the aim to intensify a man's desire by turning a secure bond, a necessity for healthy relationships, into a brass ring. Except that on the ride of Romantic Chivalry, like all carnival sideshows, the game is rigged. The brass ring remains ever just out of reach.

Men's basic human need for love, acceptance, and security is frustrated, leaving them in a perpetual cycle of deprivation.

Indeed, it is one of the core principles of romantic love to keep the bond in the realm of tantalizing denial, and men therefore in constant readiness to be manipulated and used.

The word tantalizing comes from the Greek story of Tantalus. Tantalus, as the fable goes, offended the Gods. His punishment was to be placed in a river with the water up to his neck. A tree full of ripe, red apples leaned toward him.

The Gods afflicted him with a raging thirst and hunger. When he bent his head down to slake his thirst – the waters receded. Likewise, when he reached up to grab one of the apples, the branch recoiled higher and out of his reach.

Women are socialized to tantalize men with the possibility of pair-bonding, to keep the fruit of love ever out of reach, and to further muddy the waters with the dictates of Romantic Chivalry.

If you want that pair-bond, which is to say if you want to be more tantalized, you had better greet her with flowers, hold the door open, and of course, pick up the bill.

Be prepared to live that way for the rest of your life, exiled to the river with Tantalus, ever thirsty and hungry. In modern times, simple attachment is transformed into something complex – an impulse now guided by customs of Romantic Chivalry, designed to tilt maximum power toward the woman.

Even when the pair-bond is supposedly attained, you may still experience the withdrawal of love, sex and approval as a method of control. It can even be worse once bonded than during the courtship process.

Such behavior from women is not a simple, innate reflex, but one in which they are culturally educated and socialized. Most girls become fluent in the game of inclusion and exclusion, in groups or among friends, well before they reach the age of 10 and the meta-rules learned there reappear again in popular dating advice – rules designed to meddle in the attachment security we social creatures would otherwise enjoy *sans* the manipulations.

The rules for women resonate shamelessly throughout an entire genre of literature:

- Keep an air of mystery.
- Only put in 30 percent effort.
- Make him come to see you.
- Never see him with less than 7 days' notice.
- Never call him unless returning a call.
- Never call or text immediately.
- Make him approach you.
- Don't call back immediately. You're a girl in demand.
- End call first after 15 minutes. Always. Even though it sucks.
- Even if you are not busy, pretend like you are.

Those items are the product of a cursory scan of just two internet dating sites with advice for women. They are not, however, an invention of the information age. They are the long-codified expressions of what women have been taught, from generation to generation, since the advent of Romantic Chivalry. They are obedience training basics for conditioning the romantically chivalrous man - superstimuli, powerfully effective in eliciting a superresponse. In this case, servile, blind sycophancy from weak, non-introspective men.

Romantic Love

Romantic love can be reconceptualized as a cluster of superstimuli, with each facet driving the human nervous system into over-excitement. That excitement tends to negatively impact men's long-term welfare. The damage is not contained there. Our social and familial world is disintegrating rapidly under the excesses and toxicity of romantic love. In a way, romantic love has become one of the most anti-human exploitations of human biology to ever afflict our species.

To understand where this originated, we need to take a brief look at the history of romantic love, previously called courtly love, to show that the same elements were already at work at its inception. As laid out in detail by medieval forebearers, the literature reveals the same exaggerated neoteny, enhancements of sexuality, and the same obsessions surrounding control of romantic attachment.

While the neoteny ploy has been in operation at least since ancient Egypt in the form of colored eyeshadow and eyeliners, the practice gained greater popularity after the Crusaders found eyelid-coloring cosmetics used in the Middle East and who spread the practice throughout Europe. By the Middle Ages, European aristocrats were widely using cosmetics, with France and Italy becoming the chief centers of cosmetics manufacturing, including the use of stimulant compounds like Belladonna (Italian name meaning "beautiful woman") that would make the eyes appear larger.

Thus neoteny, manufactured by artisan techniques, became the cultural inheritance of each successive generation of girls who were – and still are – taught the art of applying and then displaying makeup, especially to the eyes. Such practices probably encouraged praises of women's eyes in troubadour poetry, such as we read by the poet Ulrich von Liechtenstein in his autobiography titled *In The Service of Ladies*. There we read;

"The pure, sweet lady knows well how to laugh beautifully with her sparkling eyes. Therefore, I wear the crown of lofty joys, as her eyes become full of dew from the ground of her pure heart, with her laughing. Immediately I am wounded by *Minnie*."

Clothing, too, was always used to enhance sexuality. However, fashions didn't change much over the course of millennia and their sexual utility was not fully realized. The beginnings of frequent change in clothing styles, along with recognition of their multitude of ways of enhancing sexuality, began in Europe at a time that has been reliably dated by fashion historians James Laver and Fernand Braudel to the middle of the 14th century – a period when sexualized items like lingerie and corsets began their rise to fame.

Adding to the evidence, Jane Burns, Ph.D., details clothing's role of sexually empowering medieval women in her book *Courtly Love Undressed: Reading Through Clothes in Medieval French Culture.*

As mentioned earlier, the most powerful of romantic love's tricks was the tantalizing of men with a promise of attachment, a goal that would remain largely out of reach. Stories of the troubadours attest to a hope-filled agony that plagued the male lover, with men dwelling in a strange kind of purgatory in waiting for a few "solaces" from the beloved.

The medieval love-game went into full swing when codes of romantic conduct encouraged a toying with the two extremes of acceptance and rejection. Compare the above list of dating rules with the following list from "The Art of Courtly Love" – a love manual widely disseminated in the 12th century:

- Love is a certain inborn suffering.
- Love cannot exist in the individual who cannot be jealous.
- Love constantly waxes and wanes.
- The value of love is commensurate with its difficulty of attainment.
- Apprehension is the constant companion of true love.
- Suspicion of the beloved generates jealousy and therefore intensifies love.
- Eating and sleeping diminish greatly when one is aggravated by love.
- The lover is always in fear that his love may not gain its desire.
- The greater the difficulty in exchanging solaces, and the more the desire for them, and love increases.
- Too many opportunities for seeing each other and talking will decrease love.

Shakespeare's most romantic of plays tells the same story, with Juliet keeping her lover midway between coming and going, between stable pair-bonding and the single life. Here Juliet tells her obedient lover:

"Tis almost morning. I would have thee gone.
And yet no further than a wanton's bird,
That lets it hop a little from his hand
Like a poor prisoner in his twisted gyves,
And with a silken thread plucks it back again,
So loving-jealous of his liberty. "

To which Romeo replies, in accord with the expectations of romantic love;

"I would I were thy bird."

Following this little detour into history we now come to a final juncture of this argument, where we ask Aristotle's million-dollar question – *that for the sake of which.* To what end are these superstimuli employed?

Many would offer the clichéd answer that such practices garner "reproductive success," that the woman employing them gains a quality mate and produces offspring to perpetuate the species. But this explanation is too simple. For starters, there are other aims of human life than reproduction; such as garnering of food resources, securing wealth, attachment needs, or of securing narcissistic gratification for a woman who may never intend to have offspring – the resources garnered via her carefully orchestrated superstimuli can serve other ends.

Moreover, it appears not to have entered the minds of the reproduction enthusiasts that such strategies may, in fact, be deleterious to reproduction – all one has to do is look at the failing relationships everywhere, lowering birth rates, and decaying societies in the West that do not portend a future of success riding on the back of the superstimuli we've grown so fond of exploiting.

Narcissistic gratification is certainly one motive we've under-emphasized in our focus on reproduction, though it too is not the final motive. There can be nothing more gratifying to the narcissistic impulse than to wield power – as do most women – and to this end, superstimuli places immense power in their hands.

Narcissistic indulgence may well be a heavily socialized trait in modern women, but it also proves to be a short-term windfall with not so gainly long-term results. Evidence shows that the **misery index for women** has risen sharply in the age when they "have it all."

To summarize, the extreme gynocentrism we live with today is a freak, a Frankenstein that on some level should not be, or at least should not be any more than the super-sized Cuckoo chick that swells in the nest of a tiny finch. It's an event that our systems were not specifically designed for – yet we remain caught in the insoluble loop of desire that keeps it going.

We might think of it as a propaganda campaign every bit as strong as those used during the world wars to target our territorial reflexes, only this campaign has been in continual use and refinement for the last 900 years.

Whatever gynocentric impulse lies buried in our nervous system, it has now been supersized. We continue to supersize it with ever more refinements of superstimuli – but if we regain our awareness we might, just might, kick this Cuckoo's egg out of our biological nest. That can begin by recognizing that we have been hypnotized and deciding that we no longer wish to indulge it.

It's as simple as choosing not to chase the dragon, but to slay it.

Solutions

The Plague of Modern Masculinity

Scores of our young men today are stranded at an impasse on the road to manhood. They are bogged down in the confusion of a generation lost to treacherous forces they never saw, for reasons they were never able to comprehend. They are struggling and starving; unable to feed their souls in a world that finds them increasingly unnecessary and burdensome.

They have come of age in a time of coerced impotence, their nascent masculinity gutted and stripped long before having the opportunity to shape their character and their destiny. In that they are suffering from the loss of things never held, from things missing but never known. They are, quite literally, a lost generation of the walking wounded, wandering blindly from a battlefield on which they never knew they stood.

In that light, the path they are on is not really a road to manhood but simply a retreat from the effacing malice woven into the very fabric of their developmental lives. And it takes them not to safe ground, but directly into a dismal culture of shallowness and self-indulgence; a realm of options without obligations; of self-gratification without self-awareness or self-discipline. It is the death march of the western male, destined for a withering end ensured by intellectual, psychological and moral atrophy.

This aimless, narcissistic existence is a forced escape from lives shrouded in shame; from manhood being reduced to a Gillette commercial in the eyes of a society that holds it in contempt. All while the elders look the other way and deny it is happening. With the wholesale whitewashing by society and abandonment by the fathers complete, the newly re-engineered young man is all but defenseless against this downward spiral into terminal insignificance.

It's happening all around us. One only need look at current events to see that the world of men is quite literally circling the drain; disappearing from the stable foundations of education and employment. They are targeted with disinformation about crime and domestic violence, and about deviant sexual proclivities with women and children. These are no longer just the ruminations of twisted ideologues. The demagoguery now emanates directly from the government, backed by men with gavels, *and men with guns.* The judicial apparatus has been reshaped, not to pursue justice, but to incarcerate men at every opportunity, even to enable and encourage false accusations to accomplish that goal. This isn't just about male bashing anymore. It is about male subjugation. And it is not being executed by feminists or women, but by men.

We might proffer that the solution is a redirection to days past, when we imagine that men were masters of sacred codes; when they possessed strength and purpose and would stand against this growing tragedy and defeat it. We would be wrong. We can only find that Thomas C. Wolfe was right. You can't go home again. And what's more, you really don't want to. It was, in a sense, home that got us here. And that is a truth we must face, no matter how natural or compelling the tendency to point to any other "outside" force and satisfy our frustrations with the simplistic convenience of an easily identified enemy.

As always, our true enemy is in the mirror. The only thing that will save us is to face up to that and act accordingly.

In the fitful and often strange world of the men's movement, we attempt to answer this social malady; to create a haven, if only an intellectual one, for the refugees of this godforsaken gender war. It is a mission often hobbled by our own hands, yet the work goes on, limping toward solutions. We strive, I think, as men who have awakened, to formulate an appropriate response, and in our own way to push some sanity and balance back into the collective consciousness; to force it past the architects of institutional misandry, both male and female. But even as we exert pressure, we don't have a firm grasp on what it is we are fighting.

We have not ascertained what role traditional manhood plays in the problem. Unfortunately, what we have too often done is practice the obstinate politics of wounded children who insist that they have no role in whatever befalls their lives. We have, at times, angrily and energetically reacted to misandry, but have balked with equal vigor at seriously examining how we fostered and enabled it with allegedly masculine codes of conduct. Consequently, our efforts in this approach have failed, and miserably so. We have made some progress, and will no doubt eventually mature into a more effective movement, but not before we embrace more than the hostility we feel for perceived enemies.

Our most functional response thus far is to check out and go our own way, but I contend that an exit is not a destination. It's just a needed removal from the line of fire; a chance to collectively regroup and rethink. Remember that the young men festering at those crossroads have, in their own way, checked out, too. It isn't looking too good on them.

And it forces us, sooner or later, to swallow a pill that some will find bitter. And to face a reality that some will find unconscionable.

The feminists were right. What we call masculinity has, as it relates to modern realities, corrupt, oppressive and destructive elements that need to change.

And yes, I mean that literally.

In fact, the entire thrust of my argument is that the monstrous social degeneration we are now witnessing, more than anything else, is the result of outmoded and horribly misguided masculinity.

Of course, once we dig more than a nanometer deep into the subject, we find that objectivity and reason veer us onto an entirely different philosophical trajectory than the pathologically twisted and apoplectic mindset of feminist ideologues.

To chart our course, we will do two things that feminists never did. First, we will look at the subject without a politically driven agenda for unjustified revenge, or a mandate to dominate the other half of the population. And two, we will proceed with the sincere goal of benefit for everyone, not just an elite group.

The only sensible place to start is with a more grounded understanding of masculinity itself, something that can't be done in a 3,500-word essay, but can, with even marginally appropriate treatment, arrive at far better conclusions than the last forty years of so-called gender studies. We can rely on the combined contributions of history, mythology, politics, elements of sociobiology, and most importantly, human compassion.

In the end, we are a species of animals whose very existence depended on the development of reproductive strategies, the primary of which is that the most aggressive and powerful males are selected for mating by the most reproductively viable females. Those strategies arose from an environment of necessity and produced an effective way to produce offspring with the highest probability of survival. As a function of survival, that strategy, and not patriarchal conspiracy, shaped the male hierarchy, as well as what we now call, often erroneously, masculinity.

Some dry facts - The hierarchy of men

Despite the numerous male archetypal figures of history and legend, for the purpose of this writing, I will explore only four basic types of men. Three of the more commonly known are the alphas, betas and omegas. The fourth I will address later.

Alpha males are a very small fraction of the male population. They are highly dominant men who reside at near the top of all populations, from social groups to national governments. These men are generally characterized by the ability to force the deference of other men. In other cases, they simply have the strong leadership qualities on which human civilization has advanced and flourished.

In a sense, alpha males are either Einsteins or Frankensteins, heroes or hooligans, leaders or leeches.

Alphas sometimes tend to be obsessively controlling, abusive and megalomaniacal. If you point to any despot in world history who slaughtered scores of his own people, for the need to maintain control, or for sheer sadistic pleasure, you are pointing at an alpha male.

And yet the same can be said for the men who took us to the moon, cured diseases and accomplished great humanitarian goals.

With negative alphas, you can throw your imagined codes of honor out the window. Those codes are nothing more than tools used to force betas and omegas into compliance with their agendas. All romanticism aside, the code of the alpha male is to conquer and control, both the objects of his desire and the men he exploits and expends to acquire them. Characterologically speaking, they are a minute, worst representation of the male of the species.

They also get things done, and with great efficiency -- *if you don't consider the loss of freedom and human life.*

Incidentally, the characteristics of negative alphas are also the same ones that feminists have erroneously used to define masculinity in one broad stroke, painting all men as domineering and oppressive. Success at this enabled them to take other microscopic minorities of men and attribute their characteristics to men in general as well, e.g. abusers, pedophiles, rapists, etc.

Historically, the challengers to alphas frequently came from other alphas and often from the ranks of beta males who form the next tier down in the male power structure. Betas serve as the alpha's enforcers, the strong-arms used to maintain control over greater numbers. They also play the role of "yes men," affording them their own realm of power and putting them within striking distance (or scavenging proximity) of the alphas' position and status, including sexual primacy. Like roadies for a rock band, fortune often filters its way into their hands, and beds.

At the bottom, and most heavily populated part of the hierarchy, are the omega males. These are the pawns on a chessboard, often under the direct control of alpha, or by proxy, beta males. This is the common man, and the one most vulnerable to the hazards of common life.

A good way to look at this is to look at the military chain of command. The general tendency is that the alphas, betas and omegas shed increasing amounts of blood in descending order and claim the spoils of victory in ascending order.

Government runs in the same way. In the simplest of terms, alpha lawmakers use beta law enforcement officers to exercise their will on the generally omega population.

Or rather government used to work that way, but it really doesn't anymore.

The political sell out that changed the world

Alpha males in government didn't just collude with feminist ideologues in order to garner a sizable and dependable voting bloc. They had wives, daughters and other familial females to contend with, many of whom were supporting feminism. This effectively reduced everything to the biological imperative. Alpha males are no less, and arguably even more disposed to take whatever measures are necessary to ensure sexual status. Faced with a perceived threat to that, they effectively ceded the alpha position and became beta enforcers for the feminist agenda.

You won't find better examples of that than Barak Obama or Joe Biden, or George Bush for that matter. These alphas became the beta muscle for a feminist Mafioso, maintaining rank and privilege through enforcing ideological imperatives on the defenseless masses beneath them. They became cops hauling men to jail on the simple accusation of their wives. They became judges bludgeoning men with their gavels in corrupt courtrooms; politicians passing ever more misandric legislation; C.E.O.'s of pharmaceutical companies pushing drugs like Ritalin to sap the vitality and strength out of our boys, to make them more malleable in female hands once the father had been removed from the home.

Isn't this ironic? The alleged pinnacle of strength in the male hierarchy was exposed by feminism as the pinnacle of sexual weakness. This series of events is also a lesson in real power, and where it resides, which in the realm of sexual selection has always been in the hands of the women who did the selecting.

But an even greater irony is revealed. Women, who have bemoaned a lack of power for ages, and in fact still do, found out four decades ago that all they had to do to gain almost complete control was step up and demand it be handed over, playing the sex card as they did so. And it was handed over, by the most powerful men in the world, who in the presence of these women became like butlers offering cocktails on a serving tray.

I am not fond of that conclusion. In fact, as a man who continually struggles to break old-world ties, I am rather embarrassed by it.

Nothing learned, nothing gained

Nonetheless, what's happened here is that women, their raw biological power masquerading as feminism, have taken the dominant alpha status in our culture, and the result is quickly becoming an age of oppression and injustice more insidious and intractable than any other. It is in the biological, survival-oriented nature of women to enhance their lives through the utilization of male labor and male expendability, without compunction or moral constraint, and that is exactly where our culture has ended up on an Orwellian scale.

Defeating this monstrosity requires the insanely formidable task of battling (figuratively) through beta enforcers masquerading as alpha controllers, not to a command post with someone in charge, but through a pervasive ideology that snakes like countless invisible tentacles through the consciousness of the population at large, and that emanates from the very heart of human evolutionary psychology.

And the first strike in that battle should be, must be, at the elements of alleged masculinity that allowed it all to happen.

Meet the new boss, same as the old boss

They say there is nothing new under the sun. History reveals wisdom in those words. We can see with proper discernment that the women's movement was not really a new era for women at all. It is, on close inspection, just women and men practicing their biological strategies in a highly successful manner. So successfully, in fact, that it is rendering large portions of the male population even more expendable. So expendable that we are now creating reasons to get rid of them.

It was destined to happen once male control of the environment made it safe enough for women to start acquiring power and resources outside the traditional and protected realm of the home. This gave feminism its strongest foothold in industrialized nations founded on the rule of law. And it is why you see that law itself is now being manipulated away from the idea of justice (which was its intent in a man's world) and toward the funneling of added protection and resources to women (which has always been the intent in the world shared by both sexes).

It is not the pursuit of equality or the love of egalitarian values that has led to feminist governance, but pure blind human biology practiced in the same way it was on the African Savanna three million years ago. And the stunning successes of men making all manner of advances since then have now begun to take us out of the picture.

Quite simply, men have worked themselves out of a job.

As noted earlier, we have already begun to disappear from the ranks of the employed and educated, and the government is adopting policies to accelerate that process. In practical terms, there are fewer men needed than there once was. The ones that remain will be of increasingly lower status and will be subject to ever more draconian control.

But of course, there is one factor that will turn the tide before it's over. It is the instinct for survival. It is the only instinct stronger than sex, and it has already shown signs of emerging. We call it the men's movement; MRAs, MGTOW, even PUAs and the like. We are the evidence that men transcending biology is possible; proof that there can be something new under the sun. And we are growing rapidly because more and more men are beginning to see misandry for what it is; a loaded gun pointed directly at their heads, and at the heads of their sons.

Unlike feminism, which is simply a normal, functioning part of the female sex role advanced to destructive levels, the men's movement is the exact opposite. This is the first time in human history that an actual rejection of gender roles has begun to happen, and it is coming not from women, but men.

This is precisely the battle we need to fight. Not with women and not with feminists of either sex, but with the aspects of alleged masculinity that are leading to our destruction because they are now outmoded, archaic and self-defeating.

As we depart from the old definitions of masculinity, our first step in that direction is away from the institution of Romantic Chivalry. It may have once also been a code allegedly embraced out of the need for survival, but in the modern world, we all know it has but one meaning - female privilege.

We can now call chivalry by more modern, more appropriate names, e.g. VAWA, primary aggressor laws, Title IX, rape shield laws, Title IV-D, family court, prosecution on false accusation, media bias against men, or, if you prefer the short and simple version, *misandry*, or the hatred and fear of men and boys.

The fourth type of man - the zeta male

As previously noted, the men's movement is a unique and literally unprecedented phenomenon. It will bring with it innumerable firsts. One of them is the socio-sexual warrior, and I refer to him for the purpose of this discourse as the zeta male. The tag remains faithful to the Greek alphabet classification of other men but there is more purpose to the label.

I took it from the star Zeta Persei. I liked the navigational metaphor of the star as it is applicable in the context of the lost generation. But I was also intrigued that Persei is a direct reference to Perseus, the first of the Greek mythological heroes.

Perseus had a remarkable talent for slaying archaic monsters, Medusa the Gorgon among them, who as a mortal woman possessed great beauty, and who was self-enamored and struck with the power of her sexual allure until she was turned into a hideous monster by Athena, who later used her severed head as a weapon on her shield.

In 1940, an article by Sigmund Freud was posthumously published, entitled *Medusa's Head (Das Medusenhaupt)* in which he postulated that Medusa represented castration in a child's mind related to discovered and denied maternal sexuality.

Even more interesting is that in modern times, feminists (Women: A Journal of Liberation, 1978) adopted and reinterpreted the image of Medusa as representative of women's rage, and it served as a binding symbol of feminist solidarity.

So, Perseus, namesake of Zeta Persei, was the slayer of Oedipal shame (control) in the form of a murderously powerful, raging feminist archetype.

The zeta male.

This classification of a male is new because this is a male who until recent times was never needed. He is emergent and unpolished and struggling to find his legs, but is doing so thanks to the fertile, safe ground, provided by, of all things, other emerging zetas on the internet.

He has no allegiance to tradition or nostalgia, and in fact, is charged with plotting a new course. He cannot be shamed into control or intimidated into silence or seduced into capitulation. He doesn't fit in the classic hierarchy and would gladly bring it down in the name of his cause. When someone says he needs to act like a real man, he smiles and says, "No, thank you."

He doesn't seek power, but justice. And he has one overarching feature largely absent in the world around him. He cares about those lost young men who were ambushed coming out of the womb. And he will strive to make himself an example, living proof that there are other roads to take than the ones that lead to self-hatred and self-destruction.

Self-Respect Isn't Earned, It's Taken

The postmodern age is an ongoing crisis of self-respect for men. It's no coincidence that the men who fail to respect themselves live in a culture where the respect for men is at an all-time low.

It's impossible to overstate the significance of this. Our returning combat vets are dying more from neglect by the government who sent them into harm's way than they are from enemy action. Our overall treatment of them would be a national emergency if enough people gave a damn about men. Fact is, they don't. They are likely to see our traumatized veterans as a threat to society and as excess baggage. The truth is, society is much more of a threat to them than they are to society.

We have been watching the wholesale demonization of men on college campuses for decades, academic semesters turned into open season on men and their civil liberties. Much like combat vets in the society at large, young men in college now find the institutions they are attending have become their enemy. As academic lives, one upon another, are destroyed in the name of gender ideology, society watches and yawns.

Loving fathers enter our family court system; a system designed to treat them punitively, a system that estranges them from their children and reduces them to a paycheck, driving some to suicide.

The media, in news and opinion, continues its onslaught of lies about everything male. The parade of deceit is sandwiched between advertising that paints men as feckless incompetents who could not buy a new car or take medicine for a headache without a woman's guidance. Or worse, as we see with companies like Gillette, painting men as an existential threat to decent society.

Again, from society: Shrug. Whatever.

There is more. Much, much more; a mental health industry that considers the re-engineering of men, coerced through shame and bullying, to be good therapy. This is especially true for family therapists, whose licensed agenda is to encourage men to live with and tolerate all manner of abuse. And to humiliate them if they won't comply.

Men who are seeking to improve their self-esteem sometimes pay to have it further damaged by the sick ideologues who permeate the "helping" professions.

It is particularly fortuitous then, that "self-esteem" is largely a joke. It is nothing more than an elusive butterfly, concocted by self-help hucksters and hacks in order to keep people engaged in their services. If they can keep you chasing the promise of something that does not exist in any measurable way, they can keep you paying them to find it.

That is the only reason you hear terms like "self-esteem" from mental health professionals, and why you never hear the term "self-respect."

Self-esteem is how you feel about yourself, which is subject to change at any moment in any person under any number of circumstances. Self-esteem is impossible to measure or quantify which means in many ways that it is an utterly worthless goal unless you are in the business of selling dreams.

Self-respect, on the other hand, is about how you treat yourself and what kind of treatment you will tolerate from others. It is clearly and unmistakably measurable. And more importantly, it is completely attainable regardless of outside influences.

Anyone can clearly see and measure how they are treating themselves and what sort of treatment they tolerate from others. In short, people know when they are being crapped on, and when they are tolerating it. Failing to act on that in a self-respectful way falls squarely in the lap of the individual.

Rather than being a disadvantage, that is the trump card in your hand if you are determined to play it. Self-respect is about *your* behavior. It is about *your* choices, and I would wager to say that handing that over to the care of anyone but yourself is one of the poorest choices you can ever make. That does add a degree of difficulty because it puts the responsibility in your lap to get it done. But, of course, that is true of everything else in life.

That truth leads to an unassailable fact. You can instinctively handle most anything life throws at you if you respect yourself enough to keep your values at the forefront.

In fact, I think it more than fair to say that you could take the average man, put him through a gender studies program, send him through a nightmare marriage with a personality disordered basilisk, take his children and his assets in the divorce and drive his own family and friends to blame him for the entire mess, and his self-respect would still be within relatively easy reach.

If he has the spine to take it.

Having that spine, too, is simply a matter of choice, far removed from life circumstances.

Spine is not bestowed or gifted from others. It is not something you earn by graduating from man school. It cannot be located and delivered by a friend, a therapist or clergy. Spine is taken, without compunction or apology, and without hesitation. There is not a man on earth who can't do it, there are just too many who won't.

It should be clarified here that calling on people to find their spine is not a thinly veiled euphemism for "man up." Far from it. Women need spine, too. All humans do. It is undeniably a must in human mental health for all people to have boundaries; to have limits on how they are treated. Not having a spine does not make you less of a man, but it does make you less human and less healthy.

Once a man takes what belongs to him, namely his own spine, the battle is more than half over. Self-respect is a learned behavior. You can learn how to practice self-respect and with practice, you only get better, but if you don't go into it with an upright spine you are wasting your time.

A little secret. If you do have a good grip on your own spine, you don't need someone to show you how to grow and maintain your self-respect. And your need for useless ideas like self-esteem will simply vanish.

I am not trying to oversimplify. Much of this requires a form of courage most men have had pounded out of them from birth. This is especially true for men who have been taught to disrespect themselves — either from their families or other significant relationships stretching through the span of their lives. Add to that the way society often treats men and you end up with a lack of self-respect in men on a sweeping, societal level.

It is still your choice. And it will happen for any man who is willing to turn his back on every situation in life that demeans him. If that means kicking an abusive woman to the curb, then he simply (if not easily) must choose his self-respect over his fear of loss and/or rejection. He must let his spine call the shots and just deal with whatever emotions result from that. When the grief is over, the spine will be stronger and its value much more appreciated.

For some, it may involve rejecting the abusive treatment of a dysfunctional parent or even a dysfunctional child and rejecting any notion of guilt that goes with that kind of self-care.

Understanding the value of that can be as simple as facing the fact that a man without self-respect has little capability as a life partner, family member, father, son or even a member of society. The man without self-respect is useless to himself and everyone else.

Advice is cheap and easy to give. Nonetheless, I am going to offer some here for those who want it.

Your self-respect belongs to you. Take it. You don't need permission or approval and if you are waiting for either of those things you are missing the point. Take it! Wrest it from the hands of anyone else trying to hold it like they're a thief. Rip if from their grip and dare them to try to take it back.

If they try, deny them. Get them out of your life and don't let them back in until the battle for your dignity is over.

If you won't do that, get used to a very sorry lot in life and living with the knowledge that you have chosen your own misery. I know this is closing on a cold note. Reality often has a chilly edge.

Dealing with the Silent Treatment

Women have a lot of weapons in their emotional arsenal. One of the biggies is so common that we coined a term for it: The Silent Treatment. This is what women use in relationships to manipulate or punish men. Yes, I know. Men can give the silent treatment too. I'm sure there's a few thousand gynocentric therapists out there writing books about it. But we're talking about men here. So, if the silent treatment is a familiar theme in your life, the following pages are for you.

Of course, I can't even start this discussion without suggesting that you sit down and ask yourself what you're doing with this kind of woman to begin with. We are dealing with some harsh reality here and the reality is that the silent treatment is a weapon of the personality disordered. If you find that hard to believe, please consult Google with a query on the silent treatment. You will find that some of what you're about to read isn't particularly new, even if my suggestions on how to handle it are.

I don't make recommendations to do anything else with personality disorders other than to put them in your rear-view mirror. Say hasta la vista, baby. Show yourself that you have some standards and 86 her silent ass so she can go manipulate someone else. After all, if you don't have standards, you have no right to expectations. If you lay down like a doormat then it's unseemly to complain about a woman wiping her shoes on you.

That being said, we are not done talking about the silent treatment. What I have to say here is not about curing her of that kind of behavior, but I do acknowledge that a lot of men are from Missouri on everything to do with women. For those of you who don't know, Missouri is the "Show-Me" state. And where it concerns women, many men must be shown, sometimes a few dozen times.

If you follow my suggestions here, what you will be shown is that a woman who chronically uses the silent treatment is an emotional pathogen, willing to go out of her way to show you that you don't exist, to punish you by erasing you till she hears what she wants to hear, or gets you to do what she wants you to do. In the realm of moral poverty, she is sleeping under a bridge. But I am also going to point out that women who weaponize their silence aren't really deviating from the norm that much in the long run.

I have written copiously on how women control men by doling out attention and approval in sparing amounts. I mentioned before how the word "tantalizing" is taken from the story of Tantalus, who was sentenced by the gods to unbearable thirst and hunger with fruit and water ever just out of reach. And that is how women train men, by tantalizing them, with sex, with approval, even with communication. And they do it because it works.

Even if this is the first time you've ever read my material, you already know about this. You've seen it in women's code of conduct, putting men in the role of pursuer. It's why women expect you to be the one to call, the one to take initiative for dates, the one to pay, the one to work hardest and the one to take the physical and emotional risks. And they don't just expect to be serviced, they expect to be impressed. For your efforts, you are either rewarded with her presence and attention, or rejected. That makes women sound shitty till you consider how easily, even eagerly, most men are trained using those very techniques.

Blaming women and pointing fingers at them for the way they control men, whether it is with the silent treatment or anything else, is like blaming a hawk for swooping down and snatching up a careless, inattentive field mouse. The silent treatment is just exaggerated femininity. The only difference between that and everything else she does to control you is that the punishment aspect is more intense and overt. And it is a more direct betrayal of whatever loyalty she pretends to have to a relationship.

Like I said at the start, you have a number of ways that you can choose to deal with this, all of which should include her passing through the door marked exit, but for the sake of brevity, I will pick three ways of coping that fulfill your need to see proof.

The first is what I call the Shives Shuffle, named in honor of Steve Shives, perhaps the most groveling, obsequious man ever to engage in public life. When doing the Shuffle, you figure out what she is pissed about (or don't) and start apologizing. The apologizing is more important than understanding why you're doing it.

Remember, at her level of operation, groveling is good. If possible, though, you do want to figure out what she is mad about. If you gush apologetic about one thing, but she's really pissed about something else, then you will just be giving her another reminder of how little she thinks of you. You're just offering a little more grist for the mill and an invitation to expect you to keep groveling.

If you are unclear about the reason for her silent *tantrum du jour* (and you often will be), the best policy is to roll the dice on your best guess. Remember, she is giving you the silent treatment so you can't ask. Since you are willing to try to solve problems with someone who is treating you like dirt, then just bear with it. But please make sure you are positioned physically lower than her. Your knees are handy for that. Station yourself so that it makes it easy for her to look down her nose at you. Then start your begging with something extra servile like, "I'm just a man. I screw up so much that I have a hard time knowing when my faults have hurt you. Just know I am deeply sorry for however I offended, and I apologize for being too stupid and clueless to even know what I did." After all, if you have no self-respect, no point in holding back, right?

If you need further tips on this, I suggest subbing to Steve Shives' channel on YouTube and start emulating what you see. The proof you will get from doing the **Shives Shuffle** is that you will see her gloat over how successful she is in making you crawl and whine like a puppy for her forgiveness, whether you did anything wrong or not. If that is not proof that you are with the wrong person, then you need a lot more than this book.

The second possibility for how to handle this may be with what I call the Tat-for-Tits. This one is simple, even if it is a little stupid. Just cross your arms, stick your lower lip out a little and turn your head away from her with your nose slightly in the air. Feel the room fill with dead silence. Now, know this. While you are mirroring her narcissistic game playing, two things are happening. One, you are desperately hoping that your silence will have the same negative effect on her that her silence is having on you. And two, you are desperately hoping for that in vain.

Remember, we live in a world where women can get attention and approval without so much as lifting a finger. Men must work for it. Those who don't know any better work too hard. She knows, perhaps much better than you ever will, that your attempt to out-silence her is just another pathetic try at getting her to pay attention to you. It is a game she had the skills to outplay you at before she was five. She knows you are not ignoring her. In fact, she knows full well that you are obsessing on her much more than you were before she went silent. The Tat-for-Tits puts her just as large and in charge as the Shives Shuffle.

Both the Shives Shuffle and Tat-for-Tits are humiliating options, but if you start with Tat-for-Tits you may end up having to resort to the Shives Shuffle when you figure out it isn't working. Wham! Double humiliation! On the bright side, that double dose of rubbing your own nose into the pile of poop on the carpet will give any Missouri resident all they need to say, "OK, you showed me." And if you need more proof than a woman who drinks your personal humiliation like fine wine....

Well, don't say I didn't warn you.

And so, as you expect, there is a third option. It is the most difficult and least likely of options for men in relationships because of the internal forces that lead so many men to the Shives Shuffle and Tat-for-Tits.

To explain why option three makes sense I must go back to something I have said repeatedly. If you want to coexist with a woman in a way that does not result in making you miserable or crazy, you have to either A) Find a unicorn (best of luck to you **with that**) or B) Be prepared to choose your self-respect over her childishness immediately and definitively. In fact, if you choose B), you need to be prepared to choose your self-respect over your respect for her, which should be easy if she is shutting you out to get her way. At any rate, I call this third and final option by a simple name: The values-based approach.

Now, let me ask you something. What do your values say about your being in a relationship with someone who is not in a relationship with you? What do your values say about loyalty and work and communication that resides on a one-way street? Now, I am not asking what you would like to believe your values are. I am asking you what they really are, in practice. Because I have news for you. If you have a history of the Shives Shuffle, Tat-for-Tits or all the variables in-between, then self-respect isn't one of your values. You've no more respect for yourself than she has for you. After all, where do you think she learned to disrespect you?

To be clear, I am not saying that you must exit the relationship to have or hold on to your values. But I am saying that stepping up and taking care of what you can do for yourself is probably going to send her packing.

Don't worry, you'll thank me later.

The point here is that the moment a woman goes into silent mode, she is telling you that she has effectively checked out of the relationship. There is no communication and no willingness. So, there is, at least for the moment, no real relationship.

In my mind, the many obligations you have to her are off the table. All of them. She has cast aside her obligations to you, and you are not morally bound to keep up your end of the deal.

If self-respect is a guiding value in your life, you are morally obligated to focus all your attention on yourself and to drop the dead weight in your life. Obviously, if you have children, you still have obligations to them, but you don't owe anything to anyone who has just exited your relationship. You don't owe it to her to tell her where you are going, or even that you are going somewhere. In short, you don't owe her shit. Of course, she will never know that if you continue to act like a step-n-fetch.

This, of course, is where it gets tricky. Blowing out in a huff can be a really elaborate expression of the Tat-for-Tits maneuver. You could find yourself at your favorite fishing hole or another select recreational spot feeling completely miserable. You can do that in your own living room. The trick here is in understanding the sometimes very fine line between asserting your values and just playing Tat-for-Tits in the abandonment game. But it is an incredibly important distinction to make.

The abandonment game is one you can't win. On the flip side of that is the reality that the values game is one you can't lose unless you shoot yourself in the foot by forsaking your values. It all comes down to the same basic crossroads that I must address every time a man asks me how to handle the problems that crazy bitches bring to relationships with men. Your only hope is in your willingness to open the door and say, "Stop that nonsense or get out." Which is to say the answers should be in your hands, not hers.

Sorry, I don't have easy answers and don't believe they exist, which is why I stress that values-based living requires your willingness to let her go. If you are like most men, you will experience pangs of distress and a desire, sometimes overwhelming, to take the initiative to restore balance to your relationship.

Hear this. Anything you do born out of fear and weakness has the opposite effect of bringing balance. You can Shives or Tat your way into the illusion of balance, but that is all it is, an illusion. And underneath it is the reality that you have once again tossed your self-respect under the bus and caved into her manipulation. So, take my advice and take the pain.

The only purpose of the silent treatment is to inflict enough emotional harm on you in order to bring compliance. Matter of fact, I think I will say that again. **The only purpose of the silent treatment is to inflict enough emotional harm on you to bring compliance.** Everything else is bullshit. If she tells you she was too upset to talk, it's bullshit. If she says she was too afraid to talk, and she will almost certainly pull something like that, it's bullshit.

Everyone understands the need here and there to take a few minutes to compose yourself or to settle down before trying to resolve a dispute. That can be a healthy part of addressing problems in a relationship. But when it stretches past the point a person reasonably needs to regroup, then it ain't nothing but a ploy. Don't make the mistake of thinking it's anything else.

Now, provided she does not pack her bags, you will be presented an opportunity to put your actions into words, with her listening. She will be the one to create that opportunity right about the time that she figures out that the silent treatment is resulting in recreation for you rather than remorse. And I want you to note the importance of this crossroad for her. This is where she may, and I say *may* very carefully, be showing you that she wants to resolve the problem, or she shows you that she won't live with anything less than a lapdog. In the case of the latter, she is doing you a favor. If she opts for the former, you may have an opportunity.

Here's what you say when she opens the door to conversation again. "When you go silent, you are checking out. That is when I will check out, too. Every obligation I have to you is off the table. This isn't negotiable." Then shut up and go have some beers with a friend. I mean seriously, shut up and then find something else to do. Don't explain it further. Don't defend it and don't argue with her when she lies and says you don't understand. Or when she says that she was too angry, afraid or whatever other bullshit excuse she has for not talking to you. No matter where she tries to stray the conversation and take you off balance, and she will try valiantly to do just that, just quietly stand on what you have already said.

If she leaves, you win. If she stays and starts owning her shit, you win that round. If she stays and manages to put you back into a corner, it is only because you tossed your values under the bus, and is, in that case, your own fault.

Hopefully, you get the picture here. Winning conflicts with a manipulative loser of a woman isn't about developing a strategy and then seeing if it works. It's just about you not being a doormat. If you are not a doormat, then you won before she ever opened her mouth, or before she went silent as the case may be.

Shit Test: The 90-Day Crossroads

Ah, the first 90 days of a relationship. It's a time of infatuation; three months of emotional bliss and hot sex. It's also the precise time when men are least willing to listen to anyone about the possible pitfalls they may encounter.

And hey, I'm not knocking it. The mindless surrender to infatuation is one of the most pleasurable times in a man's life. It is days marked by little to no conflict, sex that rattles the rafters and a general state of satiation and well-being.

Of course, it will all come tumbling down, even in the best of relationships because no amount of fuel on earth can keep infatuation going indefinitely. At some point, it will come to an end and by my observation that usually comes around the 90-day mark. And the end will be signaled, almost always, by words that will fall directly from *her* mouth – in a shit test that will change the course of the relationship no matter how you respond to it.

That's important enough to say again. **At around 90 days you'll be issued a shit test that will change the course of the relationship no matter how you respond to it.** Things will never be the same after that 90-day fork in the road.

Let's start by heading upward for the bird's eye view before proceeding to the details. Anyone familiar with Red Pill philosophy will be familiar with the concept of a shit test. It's just a descriptor for how a woman tosses one kind of obstacle or another in the path of a man who is pursuing her. She then measures how he responds.

She weighs the results into her decision on whether to continue being involved with him or what form that involvement will take. It is her attempt, early on, to find out what he'll tolerate and how he'll react, especially to her less rational, more unstable side.

In this regard, shit tests are often provocative, designed to force the subject, that would be you, into an emotional quandary. Shit tests can be as unserious as saying, "Men only want one thing," testing your reaction to being playfully put on the defensive.

This, however, is not the shit test I'm pointing to here. It's nothing like the 90-day fork in the road. If you're already in the infatuation stage, you've passed these minor, introductory shit tests and you continue to pass them in between rounds of bed breaking sex and other fun times. Those shit tests are nothing compared to what's coming.

Mind you, for the nitpickers out there, 90 days is just an average. It's not intended to be taken as scientific or accurately predictive. And it's good to know that because the fork-in-the-road moment with women can come at any time. It's your job to be prepared for it.

The progression of events leading up to your critical moment will be similar for most men. You'll meet a woman, hit it off, fly through her early shit tests, rock each other's world in the sack, get along fabulously and then one day, quite suddenly, things will change.

You'll pick her up, meet her somewhere or have her show up at your door, and instead of the bubbly, smiling, carefree new companion you've become accustomed to, you will find a different person standing there. She'll be sullen to a greater or lesser degree, quiet and incommunicative; perhaps a little dark.

When you take the bait and ask, "What's wrong," she will at first give the classic lie for a response. "Nothing," she'll say, with a completely straight face.
The point here is that she wants you to be the one to force this conversation. She'll pretend to be hesitant to tell you the reason she is indisputably broadcasting her displeasure with you. She'll pretend not to know that she is throwing a wrench into your daily gears in order to provoke your inquiry and your attempt to find a solution.

And so, if you are like most men, you will jump up on your white stallion, prepared to grab your sword and shield and insist she tells you what is wrong. You'll project to the woman that you are caring enough and man enough to hear the problem and, by god, do something about it. Some men are so adept at this knightly posturing that they demand to know what the problem is and what they can do to fix it.

Rookie mistakes aside, this scenario has happened countless millions of times over the centuries. It is a standard component of every relationship based on romantic love; the kind of crazy, psychotic, chivalrous love that infatuation breeds. It is so common and so predictable that I can tell you in general terms what the problem will be before she ever shows up at your door wearing her sad clown face.

The problem will be, in one form or another, that you did something which caused her to feel unimportant or unloved. It'll be that you left a little too early the last time you were together, or that you arrived a little too late. It will be because she saw you briefly admire another woman or because you smiled a little when telling her about your last girlfriend. It'll be because you had to say no to doing something with her because of your work or because you said yes to doing something with one of your friends. It'll be about something you said in which she didn't like the tone, or because of something you didn't say but that in her opinion you should have. It'll be because you wanted to hold her hand in public, or because you didn't want to.
The point here is that at the 90-day fork in the road she is going to present you with some bullshit, some measure of her insecurity, her desire for control or both. You'll know it because you didn't really see it coming and because for the first time since you've been with her there will be a dark pall over your connection. And you will know it because you will feel the overwhelming urge to fix it and get back to the relationship you were so enjoying just moments before.

You will not be aware that your relationship, the unbridled love affair with such promise for the future just died in front of your eyes. Because gents, this is not an infatuation level shit test. It is something entirely different. And this is where I must urge you to pay close attention to what I am saying. In fact, if you haven't paid attention to a single thing I've said in this book, the time to do so is now. Because how you react to her now is going to determine how the relationship will go from that point forward. Not only that, it can decide the direction your entire life will go.

This moment, gents, is about her control of the relationship, which is to say her control of you. And mind you, it doesn't matter one whit whether she is conscious of all this or not. So, I advise you not to distract yourself with pointless inquiries about whether she knows what she's doing.

Some women are conscious of this, some are not. It doesn't make a damn bit of difference in what will happen if you screw up now. And by 'screw up' I mean take the bait and apologize or otherwise try to appease her so that you can restore the former relationship.

Again, I want you to hear this loud and clear. The former relationship is gone. It is over. It is never coming back no matter what you do.

Thinking you can change that is like trying to lasso a unicorn. Forget about it. The only value the former relationship has is to her, as an illusion to give you something to chase after.

She's dangling a carrot and nothing more.

If you fall for it and reach for that carrot, you'll just be engaging in delusion; a feeble, ill-fated stab at restoring the old, now dead, order. Take a look around you at the majority of men you know in long-term relationships and ask yourself if I'm wrong.

Men, through this very path of manipulation, have become women's autonomic relationship accessories. It's the standard of the times. What I am talking about here is the pivotal moment in every relationship that triggers that end game. There is a point, at the earliest and easiest part in the relationship in which you can choose not to go there. And the advice I have on this is pretty damned straightforward.

Whatever her problem is with the way you looked at a waitress, or the tone in your voice last Tuesday afternoon or that your forgot something she thought you should have remembered, tell her that she's being childish, and that you've no intention of defending yourself over trivial bullshit.

The first one to talk after you've said that loses.

I know that some of you are already like, "Yeah, sure, Paul. And she'll be out the door for good." And of course, you are more likely right than not. But remember what I said. The relationship you had with her is already over before you ever said a word. She's not in infatuation mode anymore, even if you are. Get that through your skull. She's in control mode and you've only got two choices. You either get out of it by directly evicting her (or running her off with your boundaries). Or you settle in for the long war.

There's wisdom in both paths. Some men already know where they fall on this. They'll say, "See ya!" and call it a day. Can't say I blame 'em.

There are also men who won't take an ounce of shit; who decide consciously and rationally that relationships with women have perks despite the unavoidable pitfalls. They believe that with enough time with the right woman, and being the right kind of man, that they can carve out something that they value and that they want. Of course, having done that myself, I don't argue with those guys either.

Both these groups, by the way, are the minority. As you know, most men, when confronted with the 90-day shit test, react to it by trying to kiss it and make it better. Operating out of fear of loss and rejection, they capitulate, which is where they end up spending the rest of their relationship, and sometimes the rest of their lives.

It's a pity. The standard for men at this juncture of a relationship is to fold like a cheap suit. Ten years later and they are sending me emails, asking for help, swearing to sweet Jesus they have no idea how things went so wrong. By then, she and the state have them by the short ones. There is little I can tell them but to brace for the pain.

The lesson here is simple. All men who live by a set of values, including self-respect, have a distinct advantage. They don't end up on their knees, crippled and confused, looking for someone to blame for how they got there.

Leading with Your Values: Every Man's Challenge

The book you are reading is geared toward a values-centered approach with women. In other words, instead of letting your dick or your heart make any decisions about women, slow down and let your values speak, particularly your self-respect. And let that self-respect have the final word.

And by self-respect, I mean self-respect on a level that you would, without batting an eye, let a *Playboy* bunny hit the road before you would tolerate an ounce of her bullshit.

The point here is that between your values, your heart, and your dick, your values are the only thing that will cover your ass. The other two have already gotten you in trouble. Strangely enough, your values, especially self-respect, happen to be the biggest obstacle to getting approval and acceptance from most modern women.

I reckon that makes it worth some conversation.

I've seen a lot of good commentary and feedback on that very subject. Some of it provides material that is perfect for penning my own responses. I got one such comment recently. This gent had the following to say about sticking to your values with women:

"The message is simple. Stay away from long-term relationships with women unless you want to jump through hoops and walk on eggshells every single day and for what?

If you follow Paul's advice and be assertive, she'll dump you and find someone who'll grovel and submit, and there are plenty of emasculated idiots out there who'll do everything that you won't do for her.

MGTOW is the only way you don't lose."

Fair enough. Every man is entitled to his opinion. I know guys personally who think this way. And it makes sense for them.

I know a lot more guys who hell or high water will seek long-term relationships. This includes men who identify as Red Pill. Like me, they won't get married, and they won't do anything else that puts them at risk of state control and abuse when it comes to a relationship, but they still seek to pair bond.

So, with all respect to the cocoon that some men can tolerate where it concerns females, I am going to interpret the comment with the much larger, pair-bonding population in mind. Let's start at the beginning.

"The message is simple," he says, *"Stay away from long-term relationships..."*

So far so good. I agree, he is putting things simply. No LTRs means avoiding the complications that come with them. It's not my way but I wouldn't argue against it.

My message is also simple, doing the bitch-ditch as soon as you see serious red flags is another valid approach, even when, no, especially when seeking a long-term relationship. After all, Red Pill men are not stupid. They are more on top of things like female privilege, entitlement whores and personality disorders than the average hombre.

While the commenter and I are not in lockstep, there is not really a significant difference between us, so far. Well, maybe there is. Let's finish that last sentence.

"Stay away from long-term relationships with women unless you want to jump through hoops and walk on eggshells every single day and for what?"

What...the...ever...loving...? Now just hold on a minute here. Bear with me, because I think that line reveals more than the writer intended.

So, men in long-term relationships *must* jump through hoops? They *must* walk on eggshells? What? They don't have a choice? Their free will is gone?

What I see in this statement is clear. He is reflecting the often-unspoken beliefs of most men. That is, you must jump through hoops and walk on eggshells *because you are afraid she will leave you.*

And he confirms that in the very next statement.

"If you follow Paul's advice and be assertive, she'll dump you and find someone who'll grovel and submit, and there are plenty of emasculated idiots out there who'll do everything that you won't do for her."

So, what we have here is not a guy making a MGTOW argument against the legal and social dangers of marriage or even long-term relationships. What we have is just a man who has raised a white flag and accepted that his values don't stand a chance around a woman. He is saying that he isn't emotionally equipped to let go of a woman who doesn't respect him.

Now, I'm aware of the fact that there are enough women who expect you to jump through hoops to elect Hillary Clinton ten times over. Entitled, arrogant women are the gold standard for the western world, and exceptions are just that, exceptions. But remember, these are not legal issues. We are not even talking about marriage, common law or otherwise. We are not talking about legal vulnerabilities. The comment I am responding to is about emotional vulnerability and nothing else.

With all respect to the commenter, I have to say that in the realm of emotions men do have choices. Building a wall around yourself is a perfectly acceptable one if that is what a man wants to do, but I don't advise projecting that fear-based decision as sound advice for every man around you.

"Oh my God, she'll leave you if you don't kiss her ass," doesn't exactly reek of a confident man.

For pity's sake, let her leave. It may cause some grief, but unless you have a ton of serious issues, it won't destroy you. There are many men who can enjoy relationships, even long-term ones, and survive the emotional fallout if the woman turns out to be a loser deep into the game. There's no reason you can't be one of them.

For any man who chooses, who is leading with his values, hoops and eggshells can be the deal breakers that show up early on. They can be instant rule outs for the conscious, non-gynocentric man. And they can be an opportunity to determine if she is teachable.

No doubt that good values will send a lot of women packing. If your self-respect is genuine, that is a lot more like letting yourself flick a booger out of the car window than being torn apart by loss.

Seriously speaking, what is it that men are afraid of losing? A hypergamy-addled, manipulative and controlling bitch? Getting rid of that is losing? How did so many men get to the totally insane and powerless point that eighty-sixing a loser with a vagina is anyone's loss but hers?

I don't have a Red Pill handbook but if I wrote one, that scenario would be in the chapter on *how you win*. Getting a loserectomy whenever it's indicated is only a loss when you have an attachment to losers or an attachment to women that is so bloody gynocentric that it will have you gobbling a shit sandwich and asking for some chips to go with it.

You can do better than that.

When I wheel my trash to the curb for pickup, I don't take Kleenex with me to wipe tears away. When something in my house breaks and I replace it, I feel good about the replacement. I don't have a sense of nostalgia or grief about the defective part. It just goes in the can with the rest of the trash.

There is only one force on earth that can make someone see cutting a female tumor out as that big of a loss. Gynocentrism. Not just gynocentrism but the equally anti-male institution of romantic love.

Romantic love isn't even a basic human instinct. It is a social construct put together by a couple of high falutin' women in the aristocracy 900 years ago. It spread like herpes in a whorehouse because men are so easily manipulated by attractive damsels.

Well, most men. That is what created the need for the Red Pill. But, just my opinion, part of the Red Pill is disabusing you of the notion that you are at the mercy of any of this. You have free will, and you have choices to make about what you won't put up with. You also have the responsibility for making those choices.

One of those choices that may be better for most men than life as a monk is to refuse to follow the psychotic path of infatuation and to refuse to confuse it with anything that might be called love.

That is a big deal. Men sometimes kill themselves over relationship losses. They submerge in booze and drugs and other forms of slow death and destructive behavior, too. Their depression during loss can be crippling.

A lot of that is because they invest the wrong things emotionally and psychologically in women and because they lack a counter-narrative to the romantic model – one that gets them through loss and lessens its intensity.

The message here is that the path to surviving loss is simple and admittedly difficult, but doable.

Lead with your values. Finish with them too. Realize that infatuation is insanity. Seek to cure it, not follow it. Romantic love and chivalry destroy your honor, your values and leave you vulnerable to great pain and abuse. There is one place that has every answer you ever needed to remain whole and healthy with women and with anyone else.

It is called a mirror. Use it often and with courage.

Arranged Marriages and the Rise of Romantic Love

There is a vast difference between the reality of romantic love and the image of it embedded in modern cultural consciousness. And it's an important matter to consider because the romantic love narrative affects every man, gay or straight, married or single, Red Pill or blue pill in this society.

Each culture has its own definitive narrative that lives in the mind of every person, in the form of stories and their associated iconic imagery. Whether reacting to that imagery with rebellion, compliance or a combination of the two, no one gets to escape the influence of the narrative.

Historical events shape all of us in one way or another. One such historical event is romantic love. The normalized, unhealthy western trend to follow the emotional and irrational sexual compulsions that come with infatuation, in pursuit of a "happily-ever-after" fantasy outcome in marriage.

The allure and power of such a model is so tempting that we see many people charmed into the pursuit of it despite overwhelming evidence that it's a bad idea.

We know, with a simple and honest examination of the historical record that marriage, without significant and even overbearing social pressure on people to stay together, simply falls apart. And, in the modern climate, it falls apart badly. It can also get rough without heading for divorce court. We know this from the incidence of divorce and from the long-term misery index of many who don't divorce.

There are some exceptions. People who stay married long enough to overcome the power struggles that happen once infatuation fades sometimes manage to attain mature love and mutual affection.

This is probably something that happened much more often when marriages were arranged, and when, for other reasons, people felt compelled to avoid divorce.

An analysis of western and eastern marriages published in the Journal of Comparative Family Studies yielded very interesting results. The article, "How Love Emerges in Arranged Marriages: Two Cross Cultural Studies," by Robert Epstein, Mayuri Pandit and Mansi Thakar (2013) reached past the obvious superiority of arranged marriages in terms of the incidence of divorce and into the arena of relationship quality based on love.

Here's a blurb from the abstract:

"The fact that love can grow in some arranged marriages – and that this process can apparently be analyzed and understood scientifically – raises the possibility that practices that are used to strengthen love in arranged marriages could be introduced into autonomous marriages in western cultures, where love normally weakens over time."

The study authors attribute the increase in love to commitment and sacrifice for the relationship. I think, however, that this is only part of the explanation. The social pressure to continue arranged marriages is likely what contributes to creating an environment where perseverance and sacrifice are possible or likely, thus creating stable, fertile ground for the growth of mature love.

Now, I am certainly not recommending arranged marriage or any other marriage for that matter. The current legal climate in the west makes any legal marriage a foolish move. I am simply pointing out that arranged marriages are far less likely to end in divorce and more likely to result in mature love than marriages based on infatuation and romance. That seems to be, at this point, a near scientific certainty.

That is information any man should consider when contemplating marriage (or why he should avoid it). Western marriage is a crumbling institution because there are no social pressures to keep it together once the illusion of romance fades and yields to reality. Those pressures ended when feminism obliterated the social stigma of divorce by getting laws changed and by lauding a lack of commitment and other untrustworthy qualities in women.

That was relatively easy to accomplish with the help of gynocentric men because romantic relationships were unstable to begin with.

Romantic love, as we know it today, isn't a human instinct. It's not a product of our evolution. Its emergence was a historical event, a manufactured and marketed alternative to arranged marriages that became a remarkably resilient social trend.

That started, as far as we can tell, in the 12th Century with the emergence of a rebellion against the stable tradition of arranged marriages.

Prior to popularizing the idea that infatuation and lust made a good foundation for marriage, an idea that in hindsight is quite insane, indulgences in romance were deeply frowned upon as acts of foolishness. Married couples could and did go through life perfectly well without it.

Author Robert Johnson writes about marriage in India, recounting a Hindu marriage rite in which the bride and groom make the solemn but hopeful statement, "You will be my best friend."

Johnson goes further. "In traditional Hindu marriage, a man's commitment to his wife does not depend on his staying 'in love' with her. Since he was not 'in love' in the first place, there is no way he can fall 'out of love.' His relationship with her is based on loving her, not being 'in love' with the ideal he projects onto her.

"His relationship is not going to collapse because one day he falls out of love or because he meets another woman who matches his projection. He is committed to a woman and a family, not to a projection."

That quote is from, "Understanding the Psychology of Romantic Love," Harper Collins, 1983.

Arranged marriages resulted sometimes, maybe often, in great fondness between husband and wife. Many may have reached a stage of mature love that can only happen with years of coexistence as life partners, but they did not start as two people head-over-heels in love. They often started as two people who had never even seen each other.

They had one other characteristic that made those marriages decidedly different than modern unions in the west. By and large, they worked. Divorces were and are comparatively rare, not because couples were in love and inseparable, but just for the opposite reason. They worked because the marriage was not in service to the fantasy of sustained romantic love.

Couples in the arranged marriage were in service to *building* love which paradoxically led to couples feeling they had more control over love and relationships. This contrasts with romantic lovers who complain about being tossed around on the waves of love with little or no control over any of it.

Romantic love is ultimately a toxic agent that was allowed to overtake the institution of marriage, partly because of the human weakness for self-indulgence and in large part because of cultural gynocentrism.

Embracing lust, infatuation and the chemically charged passions that come with them in a society that overvalues women is as easy as selling drugs. And we see the result of that when we see what happens to most marriages based on transient emotions. Once social prohibitions on divorce are removed, marriages fail like subprime loans.

We can even see the quickly mounting damage to marriage in eastern culture that has accompanied the importation of western values. The impact is a dramatic reflection of what has already been happening in the west for the past half-century.

Until the advent of gender feminism in the west, we had managed to use social pressure to keep couples together. At my age, I remember a time when people literally whispered about divorce because of the stigma attached to it. Those days have passed, and divorce is not only acceptable, but it is also the predictable outcome of most marriages, spawning entire industries in the legal, social work and domestic violence fields.

The setup for all this misery can be traced through the narrative of our past; through the imagery of romantic love that has infected human consciousness, now driving western men to confusion and often to ruin.

Most men, however, aren't comfortable too long in the skin of a victim, even when they have been victims in the truest sense of the word. When men are up against a brick wall, most tend to find a way out. We see the attempt to break free and create a new narrative, especially on the internet. And it is precisely the reverse of the revisionist feminist narrative about the sexes, casting women as slaves, chattel in a world run by and for men.

Men, a growing number of them, have begun to pen a narrative about freedom, self-awareness and self-actualization. The challenge to our failed script is a simple one. Are we willing to adopt a new one?

Can men accept a new narrative; a new vision of themselves that rejects the role of romantic vassal? Sure, they can. It happens all the time. All it takes is the willingness and the courage to embrace a different kind of self-awareness, a different, more complete history of yourself. One that does not hinge on the insane pursuit of false love and dangerously conditional approval. There is not a man reading this, anywhere, who cannot make that story unfold. The only question is whether he so chooses.

Dear #MeToo, Say Hello to #MikePenceRules

Welcome to the calamity now popularly known as #MeToo.

I wrote an essay on the current sexual assault and sexual harassment hysteria back when all the attention was on Harvey Weinstein. I did that in anticipation of all the high-profile liberals and cuckservatives who would go right under the bus as the feminist frenzy went into overdrive.

Some people felt that essay was a little heartless. And you know what? They're right. I have grown heartless about the self-inflicted blue pill misery of pompous blowhards who never gave a rat's ass about what was happening to their fellow man provided they were fat with cash and living above it all.

These are the same people, rich and powerful movers and shakers, who have buried their noses in feminist ass till cheeks met cheeks, for politics and the sake of acceptance in the demanding realm of Hollywood groupthink.

So yeah, watching these prigs fall over like so many dominoes doesn't draw tears from my eyes. Matter of fact, I am enjoying the show.

I am giddy about the outrage of Tavis Smiley, who is now railing publicly about being fired by PBS without any kind of fair hearing. He is moaning about how this, "…has gone too far," to anyone who will listen, which isn't very many people.

Yeah, Tavis, it has gone too far. And I guess you noticed this when? When they imploded your world, ending your professional life and totaling your legacy like a train plowing into a Volkswagen?

Seriously, I admire Smiley for fighting back, but just who did he think he was working for? A Voice for Men? PBS, driven in large part by our tax dollars, is one of the main players in furthering the agenda that finally hoisted him on his own, outraged petard.

And I am supposed to take pity on him?

Sorry, but I've already seen too many men crucified who never took part, by omission or otherwise, in promoting these witch hunts. And, in fact, I have known good men who went down trying to fix the problem. So, as far as I am concerned, this not only hasn't gone too far, *it hasn't gone far enough.*

And the best is yet to come. Not only are we going to get to see a whole lot more men bend over and take a great big fat one for the team in the days ahead, the payback for #MeToo craziness isn't going to end there. The real repercussions will be played out over the next generation or two.

You see, in all the mayhem, another highly relevant story has risen to the occasion. Vice President Mike Pence strolls into the landscape cool as a cucumber. As you may have noticed, the good Vice President has been complete Teflon, untouchable, even as allegations fly at everyone else.

There is no grand secret to Pence's success. The good Vice President has rules about women. He never allows himself to engage socially with them while alone. Never, with any of them, save his wife. And he won't attend any events that feature alcohol without her there, either. He is obviously practiced at this, to the point that it is woven into his standard operating procedure.

Thus, by shunning contact with women he remains Mr. Clean in the political arena, his future and his reputation protected.

Let's call this #MikePenceRules.

There have already, and quite ironically, been hit pieces on him about this in the media. The Washington Post made a retarded attempt at doing a number on him, implying that his motive for being averse to women was that he didn't trust himself around them, or some such nonsense.

The article, penned by some cuck named Paul Waldman, displayed the Olympic level mental gymnastics required to come up with the narrative.

"Let's take just a moment to consider this pair of rules Mike Pence has for himself," writes Waldman. "He obviously thinks that every interaction he has with a woman is so sexually charged that it's safe to be around them only if there are other people there, too."

No, Mr. Walderman. It isn't himself that Pence doesn't trust. It's women, and you'd have to be out of your mind to blame him.

Now, I am sure this probably made sense to Waldman, and to WaPo's regular readers, in the same way that $2 + 2 = 5$ does to that crowd. But of course, like with every other matter of sexual politics, they are all wildly off the mark.

And that is probably a good thing, too, because while they conjure up derisive, pseudo-Freudian attempts to shame men like Pence as being fearful of human sexuality, other men will pick up on the wisdom of his actions.

Vice President Pence won't be alone with women for one simple reason. It's because he knows full well that women are dangerous. It is hard to imagine anyone doubting that anymore, but for anyone who does, they can just grab the latest headline in the current news cycle. Unless we are in the middle of bombing North Korea, the headline will prove them dead wrong, and dead stupid.

I am not usually in the business of making predictions. But I've got no problem now in saying that I see the Mike Pence Rules carving themselves into the social landscape, deeply and permanently.

It's nothing new to me, mind you. I started leaving the door open 30 years ago when counseling·women with drug and alcohol problems, especially borderlines. Even in the blue pill world of mental health services, nobody questioned why I did it. They already knew.

Again, that was three decades ago. Today we have entered an age where Mike Pence Rules will be invoked across the board in all areas of life.

Of course, feminists will rage about it. *They want men in vulnerable positions* and will scream about oppressive sexism when men protect themselves, but it won't do them any good.

They will have to try, though. You see, the thing is that as the inherent danger that most women now represent becomes increasingly apparent to men, the only rational response is risk reduction.

It's not that men will just be more careful around women. It's not that men will just be more prone to covering their asses socially and professionally. It means an intentional boycott of women wherever their presence creates a risk.

The first place that comes to my mind is employment. Sooner or later, and I am thinking sooner, men are going to figure out that a woman can't file a sexual harassment charge if you don't hire her in the first place.

Now, how funny is that? For the past 50 years or so we've heard feminists bellyache about employment discrimination against women in hiring, despite the fact that it didn't happen that much.

Well, now it is going to be happening for real. I can already hear tens of thousands of employment doors quietly closing in women's faces. And, as someone recently conveyed to me, he's going to, "Slam the damn thing shut."

Here's the rub. Every time a female job applicant walks in the door, the employer, who may well be female, has two possible risks to consider.

One, if they don't hire her, she may sue them for sexual discrimination. Or two, if they do hire her, she may sue them for sexual harassment or something else along those lines.

Personally, if I am an employer, I'm going with risk number one. I'm going to discriminate against women in hiring. And I think anyone with two brain cells to rub together is going to do the same thing.

Complaints about employment discrimination are bothersome but routine. The EEOC stays busy with thousands of such complaints, most of them bullshit. Companies I have worked for in the past considered small settlements on these cases just the cost of doing business.

Getting sued for anything involving alleged sexual offenses against women is bothersome, expensive, and gets your business all over social media with something like a #MeToo pinned to the company logo. When your company gets accused of sexually predatory behavior, heads roll, investors run for the hills and the first thing the higher-ups will do is find a scapegoat to crucify. You can bet on it.

The solution is simple and easy. You take the risk on employment discrimination over being publicly stained as a rape apologist/enabler. You don't need to have Asia Argento interviewing in your office to know to leave the door wide open and file 13 the application the minute it's over. In the future, all female employment prospects are Asia Argento.

When you set aside the hashtags, fake news coverage, and the pathetic spectacle of a thousand talking heads competing to be the most outraged at men misbehaving, we have that old nemesis called the truth.

And the truth informs employers that the current hysteria wasn't sparked by women running down the street, bloody, dresses torn and pleading for help. The #MeToo Movement emerged out of the shadows, quiet and calculated; ghosts from decades past with Gloria Allred in tow, mugging for cameras and digging for money like pigs after truffles. And it leaves the true victims, the accused, no way to defend themselves in the arena of public opinion. The arena of public opinion believes the woman. Every goddam time.

That's what #MeToo is going to do to women. It's going to cut them down by the thousands without their ever knowing what happened. And as entertaining and comical as watching arrogant, hypocritical men being marched to the guillotine is, it is nothing compared to what is coming.

It's too late to put the brakes on now. Nobody need tell employers, though I happily will, that the way to reduce risk is to reduce the presence of women.

The #MikePenceRules will be written silently into their practices. It won't, of course, prevent all women from being hired. But it means with complete certainty that there is no such thing anymore as equally qualified when it comes to hiring.

Two prospective employees, one male and one female, may have near identical qualifications; identical experience, identical education, identical prospective value to a company. Identical everything, except one of them is a woman who comes with substantially more risk.

If employers are acting in the best interest of their organizations, which is their responsibility, they will choose less exposure to risk every time they can. Untold numbers of them will find a way to hire the man. A headline from money.com, December 2018, tells the story. "Wall Street's Strategy for Handling #MeToo Is Avoiding Women at All Costs." They even mentioned something called the "Pence Effect."

#HardToBlameThem

None of this is surprising. Feminism has been defined by women shooting themselves in the foot and pressuring others to do the same for half a century. They have driven literally millions of women out of the homes they really wanted to be in, out of the lifestyle and futures they wanted, and into millions of dead-end, mid-level, life-sucking jobs as corporate slaves. They've convinced women that their children are better off in daycare, and without fathers; that child support and alimony are preferable to an intact family.

And now, not content with fucking up women's old lives as wives and mothers, they have set their sights on fucking up their new lives as wage earners and taxpayers.

#MeToo, and most every other feminist initiative shouts to the world that women are dangerous and to be avoided. The consequences will damage and diminish what little women have left.

And women, writ large, will band together to make sure it happens, or at the very least remain silent in collusion. Absolutely stunning.

Mind you, I don't say any of this out of concern for women. I've no more concern for the hashtagging lot of them than I do for the likes of Harvey Weinstein and company.

I don't know how other people will handle this, but I do know my own plans. I'm making popcorn and getting ready for the ruckus. This is going to be one hell of a show.

Changing Her Emotional Diaper

Are women purely emotional, irrational human beings who cannot help but be confounded by logic? Or is there a secret wisdom in their emotions from which men can learn?

The short answer is simple. Women are emotional creatures compared to men. It's not PC to say that, along with a lot of other truths that will get you a visit from the generalization police.

I've had some men tell me that they thought it wasn't true. These are almost always the same men who take up arms against the imaginary realms of the gender wage gap, rape culture, and male privilege. I have had female feminists, too, tell me that it wasn't true, but then again, they usually had spit flying out of their mouths and were pounding a desk when they were saying it. So, there's that.

Most women are, in fact, dominated by feelings over intellect. They are often, and especially while in relationship conflict, irrational. They inhabit an emotional carnival, either riding the moody-go-round or standing in line impatiently to get on.

During interpersonal struggles, they have an unfortunate tendency to take issue with reality. They get offended by common sense and fight pointless battles against reason on their uniquely female way to solving problems by creating more of them.

This presents a fundamental problem for men. How do you resolve problems with someone who is making your problems multiply like rabbits every time they open their mouth? How do you reason with the unreasonable?

There is an abundance of advice out there, allegedly instructing men on the most constructive way to handle the emotive side of their female partners. Nearly all of it is bad.

Consider what most pundits have to say about your problems with emotionally labile women. The number one suggestion, generally, is that you must listen to your wife's or girlfriend's feelings. I am sure that is very cutting edge. I am just positive that you have never heard anyone tell you that you need to listen to and validate a woman's feelings.

We see this time and time again. We are hammered with the idea that the secret to relationship happiness resides in being a captive audience for a woman's feelings. That is regardless of the circumstances and regardless of what sort of acid is spewing from her mouth.

Here's the problem, though. None of this bullshit gets to the heart of things. These gurus aren't here to tell you how to deal with women's emotional orientation; they are just telling you different ways and reasons to put up with it in a way that keeps her, and only her, at the very center of the relationship universe. All of it, every bit, is about making her feelings the alpha and the omega of the relationship's focus.

In short, they are advising you to be an active participant in her infantilization, and to prevent your self-respect from creating any pressure on her to woman up and handle life without demanding you take on the role of emotional pincushion. The popular idea of how to deal with emotional women is to kowtow to them.

That idea, sadly the gold standard for most modern relationship advice, is driven by the mediocrity of low expectation and the assumption that your female counterpart is emotionally retarded. Personally, I can't think of anything more insulting to me or my partner.

The only antidote to this system of idiocracy requires a rethinking of some very faulty but common assumptions.

Dwelling on feelings, especially the irrational kind that tend to get worse when you point to the irrationality, is *not* a healthy emotional catharsis for women. They are not a viable communication tool that just needs your loving, patient, attentive ears to work.

What they are is partially digested, petty life disappointments which she vomits on the living room floor so that you will have to be extremely careful where you step.

Emotional reasoning is not just a woman's shortcoming. It is a woman's weapon to gain the upper hand in almost any relationship. By rolling in a train car full of irrational anger, concocted offense or spurious suspicions about your character or your actions, she is assured of putting you on the defensive and having her emotional state take primacy in everything going on between you.

She also uses this tactic to paint a target directly on your back. The self-help gurus will cheer her on as she turns her personal failings into justification to attack you.

She gains 10 pounds, and suddenly she's worried about whether you are faithful. She overspends then suddenly decides you should be making more money. She has a shit day at work, then suddenly remembers something you may or may not have said or done seven years earlier and decides that she is just now getting around to expressing her displeasure with you.

That is what most men end up dealing with, and that is the dirty little secret that most people giving so-called relationship advice won't bring up when they are wagging fingers and telling men how they need to listen to their women's feelings, without judging, criticizing or trying to fix them.

Being a crazy woman works because being a normal man, you are likely to turn somersaults trying to restore her sanity. If helping her regain her sanity is one of your priorities, it may help you to notice that her sanity usually returns when you take the blame for whatever she wants you to, or as soon as she gets her way about whatever it was she wanted.

The advice to sit there like a chump and say "tell me more about your feelings" translates to nothing less than "Please smash me on the head with that hammer a few more times. My head is not bloody enough."

If you want a life as an emotional doormat, then deify your woman's emotions and trust there is some grand wisdom in them, even when she is acting like a four-year-old pissed off because the candy jar's out of reach.

After all, it is your life, and no one has a gun to your head.

Now, am I saying don't listen to a woman's feelings? Of course not. I am saying, however, that if you have a single clue about what is good for you, you will put a limit on it.

When men have a bad day at work, what you are likely to hear is something like, "My day sucked. Sometimes I want to strangle my boss." And then it is over. Time to crack open a beer and unwind, usually talking about nothing at all, but certainly not talking about their shitty boss. Men don't typically want to relive what sucked the first time around.

When women have a bad day, what you are likely to hear is two hours of her droning like bagpipes about how Wanda in accounting is a bitch. You have heard the same bellowing a dozen times before. It is starting to sound like fingernails on a chalkboard, but alas, women's feelings are sacred, and it is your job, by God, as a real man, to indulge her because she can't quit obsessing on people she doesn't like.

With this in mind, what they say about women not wanting you to fix their problems is usually bullshit but it is sometimes true. When the problem, at least in her mind, is you, which it almost always is, you can bet your ass she wants you to fix it, even if it kills you in the process, and even if the problem is really her.

When the problem is not you, which is admittedly rare, she does not want you to fix it for her.

She doesn't want you to fix it because then she would have to shut up or find something else to talk about. What she wants is for you to set aside everything (including any desire you had to decompress from your day) and listen to her gush out her feelings until she wears herself out talking.

If you make the mistake of getting tired of that, then you are a bad partner. Then she will need to talk about her feelings about *you*.

In short, it is all about control. It is all about the world revolving around her. Her day, her feelings, her issues. Your job is to treat her like an emotional toddler and sponge that crap up till she is satisfied that the moon and stars once again revolve around her.

It's a shit way to live for any man who possesses an ounce of self-respect. But of course, most men specialize in living shit lives with a highly negotiable policy on self-respect.

Those men interested in something else, however, have options.

The best thing for life problems like this is almost always preventative medicine. I estimate, in ways that are embarrassingly unscientific, that there is about 20% of the female population who process emotions in a more masculine way.

Perhaps it has something to do with in utero testosterone flooding. Maybe it is just the luck of the draw, but there is a population of women who don't need a feelings marathon every time the grocery store clerk is rude to them, or because Wanda in accounting managed to hook some guy in senior management who drives a Porsche.

Or because, God forbid, you're not perfect and sometimes prove it.

And yes, by the way, I am saying that at least 80% of women are emotional reasoners, and in their raw state are unfit for intimacy, consistent communication, problem-solving or being anything other than a life sucking pain in the ass. Of course, I must add that at least 90% of men deserve that kind of treatment. They prove it by tolerating, no, begging for it.

Self-obsession and the insatiable need for an emotional repository in Levis is an obvious trait in those afflicted. It even shows itself in the honeymoon period, during which almost all women will bring you some crises, then time how long you remain transfixed on "being present," which is another way of saying being glued to her emotional story as though it was an episode of *Game of Thrones*.

If she's not wearing the t-shirt that says, "less you, more me," it's probably because she's worn it out. If you don't want that emotional toddler a year into a relationship, don't start out by getting involved with one.

There are ways, however, to reduce the chronicity and severity of some of the remaining 80% of women. It's a little bloody and a little brutal, but it is doable except for those at the Angelina Jolie end of the emotionally whacko spectrum.

Thankfully, there are some women who process emotions in a more masculine way. But what of most women, the ones whose lack of emotional acumen can have you stepping on a mine before you even know you're in a minefield? What do you do if you are already involved with this kind of woman?

The answers to that are simple, but we need to get something straight from the outset. Previously, I used some quick examples of what passes for advice on relationships. I also pointed out that it was all bullshit. I didn't just do that to have some fun at the expense of others.

The fact is, and by fact I mean my opinion, the entire relationship coaching and advice culture is one big, gynocentric load of crap. Pick any popular book or video series on salvaging relationships and what you will find under the misleading cover is advice on how men can keep women happy. That's it.

From start to finish, those books are written to profit from the message of pleasing women. That is why only women buy them for the most part. Their advice has nothing to do with healthy relationships and everything to do with assuring women that men are supposed to be comfortable in the role of a conscripted emotional vassal.

The biggest problem with that, aside from the lopsided agenda to infantilize women and make servants of men, is that *it's a woman's job and her responsibility to attend to her own happiness.* Most relationship advice undermines her ability to do that; a fact conveniently ignored because personal accountability makes the average woman close her purse faster than a man without a job.

So, we are left with a glut of advice on how to give women what they want, the subtext being how to make sure they keep an interest in you; how to make sure they will still have you.

The fact that I'm a lot more honest than that means two things. One, a much smaller audience for me, and two, you get to hear something other than a string of lies.

The first bit of truth is probably the most brutal. There is no how-to formula for any of this. There is no set of behaviors, no game, no techniques that will make an emotional reasoner somehow find rationality and maturity.

When dealing with a destructive, emotional reasoner, there is no chance of improving things that doesn't also come with a significant chance of ending the relationship. If you can't handle that, you might as well stop reading now.

In fact, if your goal is to fix her and in fixing her, keep her, then you are on the wrong path.

The only objective I can recommend is to learn how to build a psychological and emotional wall between yourself and her craziness. And you do that through two key absolutes. The first is your willingness to detach and immediately invest in something other than her when she refuses to reason. The second is your uncompromising willingness to let her go if she can't handle what you did first. This can be any female family member, friend or acquaintance of either sex, not just your wife or girlfriend.

If you are like most men, you are ultimately looking for little more than a relationship that does not destroy your peace of mind. You are not looking for a happily ever after fairytale, or life in La La Land with your princess. You'd simply like to have a decent, peaceful and God forbid harmonious coexistence with your wife or girlfriend.

You don't want drama over infantile bullshit, and you don't want to spend time on the perpetual hamster wheel of seeking her approval.

If she happens to be an emotional reasoner, a destroyer of the peace, then your only viable recourse is to deliberately face your fear of loss, then quietly and resolutely draw a line in the sand.

If you balk when she threatens to leave, all you have done is increase her sense of power over you.

Make no mistake about it. Even though you are not saying the words directly, you are issuing an ultimatum. If she wants any kind of relationship, communication or support from you, the crazy shit must pack its bags and head for the airport.

Not to belabor the point, because this is a point you can't belabor, you cannot motivate change in a woman's behavior unless you are willing to kick her to the curb. If you want to hear something more comfortable than that, then Dr. Phil, John Gray, and a thousand other gynocentric clones will be happy to have you buy their books.

I know this is rough stuff, but rough stuff is the only thing I know that will have the slightest possibility of helping you find peace with or without a woman. So, if you need sugarcoating, get a donut.

I now want to issue a reminder that this is not about changing her. The point is to change you, which is the only thing you can change.

She may well change if you follow these suggestions, or she may hit the highway. In fact, I am betting if you follow my suggestions closely, one of those two things will happen. But the fact is that it takes two to salvage a relationship. The only thing you can salvage on your own is you. Remembering that every day will make this a lot easier.

You can start this with what I call the Terminator Move. When there is conflict, the moment you realize you are not dealing with a person who is willing to reason, quietly inform her that you will be ready to listen when she can be reasonable and mature, then go stream Arnold with your headset on.

If you had any plans with her, cancel them, unless it is something you must do, like a medical appointment or a funeral. Whatever you do, whatever she says or does, you must ignore her and find something else to do.

If you are like many men, this is easier said than done. Some men will be angry and find it difficult to resist the fight. Others will be yearning for a sense of balance that can only come from resolving the conflict. For most, concentrating on the movie will be difficult.

Of course, the movie is just a metaphor. The point is that you must withdraw from the conflict with the clear message that you don't do irrational bickering. Spend some time invested in anything but her.

That time is best spent examining and questioning your state of mind and your feelings. Challenge yourself on your desire to fix things with the very person who is making that impossible. Ask yourself why you continue to seek solutions with someone who shoots down every rational option you offer.

Allow yourself time for your intellect to override your emotions, which prevents you from trying to make her see reason. She won't. And time for you to quit obsessing on the possibility that she may leave, which might well happen.

Remain detached until and only until she demonstrates the willingness to be reasonable.

By reasonable, I don't mean until she agrees with you. These suggestions all presuppose that you are rational and fair with her. If you are not, you have a whole other set of problems that I cannot address in the scope of this book or ten books.

Now, some men will say that they can't get away from her. They don't have a man cave or a place in the home where she won't follow them, continuing the conflict. If that is the case, get out of the house for a while. Go to a movie. Go to dinner. Visit a friend if she hasn't run all of them off. Take a long walk.

Freaking FIND a way to escape. Don't make excuses. Take responsibility for getting her out of your hair. It's your job to prove to yourself that you don't do crazy, repeatedly, till it starts to sink in on both of you that you don't do crazy.

Once again, that is the point. The repeated, proven message that you won't participate in irrational, stupid, emotionalized arguments with a child posing as an adult will certainly put her at a crossroads, but the onus to learn is still on you. If she is smart, she will realize that the only path to resolving her complaints is through acting like an adult.

"You get what you tolerate" is not just some catchy cliché that looks good on an internet meme. It's a fact of life you are much better off facing.

The Terminator Move is not for her benefit. It's for yours. The ability to detach and take care of yourself, and to practice the good value of not arguing with a capricious child can save your sanity. It is your willingness to be alone and to pay whatever price you need to pay for hanging on to your dignity that allows you to set limits and maintain them for the rest of your life.

And that is it on this front, amigos. There is nothing else to it. The tough part for most men is that they are so conditioned to ultimately yield to a woman's desires, no matter how childish, that they end up miserable. Sometimes, all too often actually, they end up suicidal.

It also contributes to problems with drinking, drug abuse, affairs and even violence out of the frustration. All of that can be eased, even cured, once you expect nothing more of yourself than to be a fair and willing partner vs. being tethered to her whims like an unpaid butler.

To beat the dead horse one last time, all of this is up to you. The responsibility for all of it is yours. You can make her change her own emotional diapers if you are not the one standing there with a handful of baby wipes every time she makes a mess.

Male Space is an Inside Job

Throughout the network of modern men's media, you will find a substantial amount of perspective on the concept of "male space." There is a lot of harsh commentary from men who feel male space has been encroached upon by women, and by gender ideologues who believe that male occupied space is inherently dangerous.

This certainly would appear to be the case when you consider many traditionally male institutions that have been forced through legal channels or coercive publicity to relent and include women in whatever they are doing. This even includes what some might consider privacy violations, such as female reporters being allowed into the locker rooms of professional athletes while they are in various stages of undress.

Some men point out, and rightfully so, the hypocrisy of this happening in a society which has had an explosion in women's organizations that routinely exclude men. And as is the traditional rule, male reporters won't be finding their way into the dressing rooms of female athletes unless they want to be arrested.

Sadly, this is usually where the conversation stops. There is little explanation to be found of what constitutes male space, or why it is so important. With all respect to those writing on this subject, it too often falls short and lends itself to victim mentality. It's understandable. The hypocrisy is real, as is the dearth of male space. Still, I want to attempt to take a deeper look at what is happening. As always, you're the judge and jury.

In the mid-1990s I worked at a residential treatment facility for men, women and young adults with alcohol and substance abuse problems. The campus was nestled in a locally iconic pre-midcentury residential area surrounded by sprawling oaks that were planted when the homes were built.

In addition to a nursing station and an administration building, there were three homes, two for men and women respectively and one for young adults.

The men's home had a covered back porch with ample seating. During good weather (and sometimes bad) the men occupied that area, working on written assignments, reading or just talking with each other.

It was no coincidence that they chose this area to congregate. Just next to the porch railing was an outside stairway that led up to where the women were quartered, on the second story of the house next door. Every woman coming or going from there had to pass by within just a few feet of the men's porch. That often resulted in the women stopping to chat with the men. Sometimes briefly, sometimes longer.

I spent time observing their interactions. When women were not present, the men remained focused on what they were doing. They were generally loose and comfortable. Most importantly, they appeared comfortable in each other's company.

When female clients came by, particularly the attractive ones, everything changed. Reading and writing ceased. The men's posture immediately improved. Occasionally chests puffed out, and some men stood upright as if to take a more visible position among their peers.

In most cases the men who were sitting and talking with each other disengaged and put their focus on the woman. In more fundamental terms, when the women showed up, the men immediately abandoned whatever they were doing, and entered a competition with each other for female attention.

The more sexually attractive the women, the more competition and the more tension between the men. Those occasions were sometimes marked by conflict and arguing among the men.

This was not an invasion of male space. The men were, instinctively, reflexively competing, even undermining each other and betraying friendships in order to draw the women into that space.

I decided to use this as an opportunity for an experiential exercise for the men, starting in the weekly men's group I facilitated. In that group, I recited some of my observations to the men about what I saw. The anxiety level in the room immediately went up. Clients fidgeted, shifted their weight around in their chairs and stared at the floor.

We were already in uncharted territory for most in the group.

I gave them an assignment to carry out before the following week's group. I told them that while they were on the porch, the objective was to remain focused on whatever they were doing and not interact with the women who came by. They were to be polite but explain to the women that they were busy and did not have time to socialize, then to go back to whatever they were doing.

The anxiety level in the group spiked again.

I inquired about that and the responses I got were mostly an acknowledgment that the men feared their actions would be interpreted as rude and the women would be angry. I took this to mean, and still do, that what the men feared was being rejected; that it was not about offending the women so much as losing their attention and approval.

I sent the men off, some of them looking sheepish, to tackle this assignment. I was not convinced that they could or would go through with it.

I came to work the following Monday and the first thing I was greeted with was another staff member telling me that the women were complaining that the men had been rude to them over the weekend. I regarded that with some suspicion, which was later confirmed by talking to the men in the community. To the last man, they all maintained that everyone had been polite but had followed through with the assignment.

They also confirmed that the women had become angry. In fact, a couple of them had tested the limits by lingering near the men's porch. When that failed the anger bubbled to the surface. Interestingly, and to my surprise, the men reacted to this by firming their resolve. Eventually, they moved back into the house where the women were not allowed.

The exercise yielded some interesting results. One, I did not anticipate the women's anger, though in hindsight I probably should have. The other is that not only did the men follow the instructions, but they also became determined not to be defeated. They grew closer to each other and for at least that weekend the arguments and conflict that typically happen between men in those settings dropped to near zero. They had congealed as a group and were working together, arguably on the problems that brought them to treatment in the first place.

Instead of surrendering their space, they created it and built a fence around it as brothers.

Another interesting effect was the one this experiment had on the clinical and administrative staff. Some of the women who worked there were offended. They thought that the exercise I gave the men had nothing to do with their treatment for addiction and that it was hurtful to female clients. I recall that the word "abusive" even came up. Some of the male staff felt the same way, though male and female staff alike were unable to articulate any form of reasoning about it that made sense.

Their inability to do that was understandable. They were trying to express emotionally driven objections; an irrational rationale. The attitude was the same brand of obtuse that we find in people who think it was women's oppression that kept female reporters out of men's locker rooms and that men banding together, focusing on their own needs and the needs of their male peers was harmful to women.

Frankly, at that point, the staff was lagging the male clients on emotional health and insight alike. The men, with few exceptions, gained from it. Several of them described the experience as "empowering," an interesting word from the mouths of men.

I could see it in their demeanor as well. I found it intriguing that it expressed itself in some of the same ways that I saw in the men when they were posturing to draw feminine attention. Their posture was better. They walked more upright with an air of confidence atypical to men in that setting. **They were projecting the demeanor they projected when trying to impress women, but they weren't trying to impress anyone.** I will wager that for some of them it was the most genuine self-respect they'd ever felt in their lives. They exchanged knowing glances and smiles with me for quite some time.

At least one of the men in that experimental group was gay and he reported the same benefit as the others, plus he felt more included as a fellow man than he had before.

All the men felt better about themselves, something incredibly important for people who have wrecked their self-respect with alcohol and drugs. They learned about themselves and about men. Oh, and a thing or two about women as well.

Men change when you bring a woman into the picture. They change rapidly and visibly. You can have a group of happily married, committed men in a group; men with no intention at all of infidelity, and when you introduce an attractive woman in the picture, they can turn on each other. They lose focus on whatever had them previously occupied. They compete. It is instinctive. It is nature. And it affects all men.

Is this a suggestion that men should avoid women? Hardly. Human beings pair bond. It is not nearly always for life, but they still overwhelmingly tend not to fly solo in life. Their healthy, normal needs include intimate connection.

For men, just as it does for women, it also means a time and place for space of their own.

We may not be able to control whether women are allowed entrance to a men's country club, or into men's locker rooms or any number of other places. Each man and each group of men can, however, take the space they need to connect to themselves and to each other. Those who are offended by that are just those who want irrational, exploitive control. The kind of control women are accustomed to having over men.

That is what the staff at a treatment facility found offensive. Men turning inward and doing the very work they were there to do; connecting to each other supportively in the process. They were concerned that men doing this, that men getting healthier, better, was an affront to women. For them, the men's actions on that porch was a problem to be fixed rather than what it was, men in trouble supporting each other and restoring some of their dignity. They were isolated, disaffected men finding connection and a sense of community.

Men's challenge is not to defend male space, but to create it. Male space, the kind that matters, isn't just in the brick and mortar world. It starts with the sanctity of their own minds and hearts. It is in the ability to tend to their own needs rather than blindly surrender to reproductive instinct, laying waste to their dignity and leaving their brothers under the bus along the way.

It cannot be taken. It cannot be encroached upon. It can only be surrendered.

Bemoaning the lack of male space is not an act of dissent. It is not activism. It is simply an acknowledgment of personal and collective failure.

When men value themselves and brotherhood more than an approving smile from a pretty face, they will have all the space they need.

Lessons in Accountability from
My Marriage and Divorce

A long time ago, in the galactic stupidity of my youth, I married a woman. Good god was she ever a piece of work. She lied like she had cancer and lying was the cure. She snatched up every dollar I earned and dropped it directly into the black hole of her self-indulgence. She elevated being irrational to an art form, especially when she was called to account for anything. She was an entitled bundle of needs, wants and musts with big tits and a bigger sense of entitlement.

I was driving heavy haul at the time, pulling oil rig components up into the mountains of Colorado and Wyoming. I drug 100,000-pound loads up pucker-inducing inclines and around endless switchbacks, on six, sometimes seven axels. Each climb up had a similar view; walls of rock on one side and stomach-turning drop-offs on the other. I'm talking bona fide white-knuckle shit, guaranteed to make you look for a deal with Jesus no matter what you believed on flatland.

After the rig components were delivered, I'd shoot back to Houston for loads of drill pipe and run them back up the same way. Meanwhile, my wife was back home loading some pipe of her own.

Of course, and to no one's surprise but mine, it all fell apart. I found out what she was doing, which was basically breaking all the rules and breaking the bank while I was breaking my back at work. I was flattened by the cruelty of it, and by the lack of conscience. I've seen vultures with more remorse. I wanted to know how it could happen. So, like an idiot, I asked.

Of course, she figured it was all my fault, being as I spent my time away from home having all that fun. Somehow, she failed to make the connection between my 12 to 14-hour days on the road and her closet full of clothes and accessories. She reckoned I was a bad husband who made her have sex with other men, at least when she wasn't squandering all my money. Poor thing didn't have a choice.

Now, at this point, I must admit that I was stumped. I was trying to understand how this was on me, but I just kept drawing a blank. Not that it mattered, though, because it wasn't long after all the poop hit the fan that the lawyers were called in. That's when I found out that the worst of the lying, stealing, damseling and dirty dealing was still ahead of me.

If you think a woman can be a lowlife bitch during a marriage, just try one on during a divorce.

I won't even bother with all the details. Suffice it to say I was lucky to get out of it with my ass still attached to my body. And my ass was about the only thing I came into the marriage with that I still had when it was over. My money, my heart and my faith in justice were history.

I was lucky in one way. I got a lawyer who didn't lie to me. I know what you're thinking, but it's true. I stumbled onto an attorney who looked me square in the eye and gave me the uncommonly sound advice to skip the expensive fight, the costly, futile quest for justice, and give her what she wanted. He told me, matter-of-factly, that I was going to lose it all anyway. After all, this was Texas and I had a penis. It wasn't a good idea for me to get cocky.

A thousand bucks went to the lawyer and everything else, including the better part of my sanity, went to her. I was a free man.

Well, free is a relative word. I was divorced. I no longer had her there making me miserable. I was doing a bang-up job of that on my own. The story of my marriage and divorce kept playing out in my mind like a stupid song that you hate but can't get out of your head. It stayed with me like a bad cold; there when I tried and failed to go to sleep at night, and there the moment my eyes opened in the morning.

It was there when I put food in my mouth that I was too distracted to taste, and when I hung out with friends, too miserable to have a good time. It was there when I was back at work on the highway, stuck with my unpleasant memories and the sound of my wheels turning, feeling angrier and angrier with every passing mile.

My life, or what was left of it, was a hot mess.

There was something else going on; something nagging at me through the angst and heartbreak; a kernel of wisdom hiding in some dark corner of my mind. It was waiting there for me, ready to show itself when I was ready. But, of course, it was a long time before I was anything like ready.

Alas, time can be a great healer. Enough of it can put most anything behind you. And for me, a couple of years of driving and fuming helped to cool down the pressure cooker of my life. Somewhere on the road, it was outside of Denver, or Cheyanne, I don't remember which, it hit me. Like suddenly the light switched on, whether I wanted it to or not.

The bitch I married was the bitch I married. That was the truth about my wife that I really didn't want to look at. *I chose her.* I opened the door and invited her right into my life. There wasn't a gun to my head. Nobody was twisting my arm. I picked her, pursued her and stayed with her a long, long time after I knew better.

Sure, there was a honeymoon period where she was all love bombs and blow jobs; where the darker parts of her nature were kept on some measure of a leash. But if I am going to be honest, and I mean the kind of honest you can only be after you bottom out on self-pity, there were a thousand red flags there that I knew about and chose to ignore. Or rather that I chose not to see, even though they were all planted squarely in front of my face.

From the time I met her till the time we said, "I do," I had never seen her own one single bit of her behavior. She'd never been accountable for anything. That extended past our relationship. She had given me, early on, a narrative of all her other relationships, painting herself every time as the victim. She had told me all about the string of horrible bastards with whom she'd been involved, and I had elected to not know that at some point I was destined to become one of them.

She was selfish, childish, and eternally demanding. When we had conflict, she had to win, even when she was completely wrong, and she knew it. It was clear she thought the world revolved around her, or that at least it should. And, of course, I just wrote this off to her being a woman. I considered it par for the course with women, which is true, but I let normalized selfishness in women overshadow the fact that I accepted that norm without question. I willingly took a bad deal, a deal that was bound to burn me, because I figured everyone else did. And because I wanted her to want me. I resigned myself to a patently unfair arrangement without lifting a finger to stop it.

Whether or not these dangerous features of personality were typical for women, I still made the choice to ignore them; to look past them, because her acceptance of me, however transient, was all I was interested in. It was all that mattered. It was me saying that I didn't matter. And it was me acting like it.

It's a humbling experience after two years of moving a mile a minute, beating the steering wheel and raging like a madman, to wake up to the fact that the only thing that had happened, the only thing that mattered, was that I got exactly what I paid for. I entered a relationship like a simp, and I got treated like one. End of fucking story.

I didn't know it at the time, but that moment, that epiphany on the interstate, was my first true Red Pill. And it was simple. The moment I saw myself, honestly and clearly, in the harsh light of reality, I knew I never wanted to see myself the same way again. I spent two years feverishly trying to figure out what was wrong with her, only to find out that the problem was me.

I still think of that moment from time to time, especially when I hear from men who are convinced that they are victims; that they aren't allowed to hold women to account; that they can't take care of themselves. Especially with men who swear up and down that they had no way of knowing what they were in for.

And I get it. I would have sworn to the very same thing if you had asked me before that day. And true to life, some men do get taken totally by surprise. I just can't say I've ever known one.

Men's most redeeming feature is their ability to own their shit. It's the capacity for accountability that we so feverishly socialize out of women's way of thinking. It's one of our advantages over women, and it would be a lot more useful if our gynocentrism weren't such an Achilles Heel.

Under the influence of gynocentrism, we not only fail to see where we are responsible, we often think we're responsible for things we're not. We end up taking on a lot of crap that doesn't belong to us. We can be convinced that we're to blame for being abused because we didn't do this or that enough, or didn't do it right, or at the right time in the right way. Because we said the wrong thing or because we didn't say the right thing. Because we didn't make someone happy who is constitutionally incapable of happiness.

We blame ourselves for the mistakes and misdeeds of others. And, of course, by others I mean women. We don't practice this ridiculous self-flagellation with other men.

With women, we can work tirelessly for them and then accept blame for not being home enough. There is no shortage of women whining endlessly about husbands who are married to their work, but who would be gone with the wind in a heartbeat if he slowed down and dared to make less money. Remember, my exes' excuse for an affair was that my taking care of her took me away from home.

Men are vulnerable to this garbage because the synergy of our accountability and gynocentrism produces a tumor. In that cancerous condition, we refuse to hold women accountable. We're also bent on pretending that a turd is a rose.

The resistance to dealing with that is understandable. If we held women to account, most of us couldn't stand being with them for more than 10 minutes. And they wouldn't think much of being with us, either. It's hard to find femininity and accountability under the same roof.

If men held women to account, a lot of marriages and long-term relationships simply wouldn't happen. Subsequently, a lot of divorces wouldn't happen either. A lot of misery, a lot of heartache and a lot of loss would be prevented.

And in case you're wondering, that is the point. As men, our ability to hold our own feet to the fire is the best friend we'll ever have. And our failure to do that where it concerns women is our worst enemy. Worse than the state. Worse than family courts. Worse than feminism. Worse than gynocentrism itself.

Our choices are accountability or victimhood. And as I have said so many times before, the Red Pill path forces us to accept that there are no victims, only volunteers.

Playing Your Own Role in Life

"Freud drops the empirical disguise and we see him as a writer of pure fictions. Ever since, we are all, in this field of psychotherapy, not medical empiricists, but workers in story." ~ James Hillman

I write frequently about personal story, about history and narrative and how those things go into shaping everything in our lives – the good and the bad. It is sometimes a difficult concept to get across. Most men have a healthy reliance on straightforward sensibilities. We approach our lives practically and use logic and common sense to solve problems. At least outside of our relationships with women, those things serve us well and reliably to navigate through life.

For the sake of personal experimentation, I want to ask you to consciously suspend some measure of disbelief and participate for a short time in a more transcendental pursuit. We could even call this an exploration in the realm of fantasy. And, indeed, for our purpose here, that is precisely how we can look at our lives - as works of fiction, incomplete and in need of editing.

Or like a series of images that spell out our history and self-perception. Some of those images are clear and dominant, others are faded and barely visible. Or, if you prefer to imagine this in literary terms, parts of our narrative are dominant while other parts fade and are sometimes lost or forgotten.

To help illustrate this a bit more, I am going to borrow from family systems work and birth order mythology. While there is nothing particularly scientific about this, and many exceptions to the birth order mythos, people often find there are stereotypical birth order traits that personally resonate in their lives. And there is some science that would seem to support those perceptions.

A 2007 Norwegian study, for instance, concluded that firstborns had two to three more IQ points than children born after them. That is according to Dr. Frank J. Sulloway, author of "Born to Rebel, Birth Order, Family Dynamics, and Creative Lives."

However interesting that may be, we won't, as in the quote from Hillman at the start, busy ourselves so much with science, but with the transcendent power of our imagination. It is the story, and under whose control it is told, that matters.

The birth order traits in three offspring are, in descending order, roughly as follows.

The first born. The hero child. The role of this child is as the bearer of the family's honor. He is the good student, industrious, and accomplished. He gives the family a sense of pride. He often goes on to success in life. And he becomes the standard to which his siblings are held by the parents. They either do this overtly or covertly, but the message is clear. The hero is where the bar is set.

Underneath the accolades and visible accomplishments, there is often a quiet form of misery. The hero child sacrifices their identity in order to fulfill the role of hero. They forsake much of what they desire for what they perceive the family of origin needs.

The middle born. The lost child. The role of this child is to lessen the load on the family by not having needs. They tend to be loners, disconnected from others. They may train themselves to believe they don't need people. You can't punish the lost child by sending him to his room. That is where he usually wants to be anyway.

The last born. The scapegoat child. The role of this child is to bear the families sins, as it were. He is the rebel that points, often wildly, to the elephant in the room. He is the one who acts out and the one the family burdens with all their unacknowledged dysfunction. He lives in a world of pointing fingers, blame and often abuse. He tends to react to those things with defiance.

Again, these are very simplified versions of these roles. Birth order roles don't always follow birth order. They can be affected by sex and other factors, and they can change with time. There is overlap between roles as well. It's a very fluid situation.

But chances are that most men can read about these three simple roles and find themselves somewhere in the mix. They can identify with the imagery of at least one of them. What happens, though, is that the iconography of the life story often becomes fixed, narrow and limiting.

For example, the hero can be trapped in a single image. Imagine the attorney or the businessman who watched his secret dreams of being a musician or woodworker fall away from the pressure of giving the family their trophy son. Imagine the possible resentments that were buried alongside a good bit of his individuality and the unspoken stresses of carrying the family weight from the time he was born.

Think of the lost child, who trains himself to the impossible task of being needless, of forsaking human connection and interdependence because his single image of life, his only story, is of not being a burden. Imagine that the cost of any relationship outweighs the reward. And imagine the countless number of unseen possibilities, the life gifts never realized simply because the lost child, in order to survive their loneliness, develops the belief that the gifts are not needed.

Finally, consider the scapegoat, as the possibility of family connection slowly fades from life as he accepts an image of humanity that cannot be trusted. There's one benefit for the scapegoat. Of the three roles, he is the one who is most likely capable of escaping. But at what cost? And what becomes of his chances for his filling a different role in life?

The point here is that in each of these roles, the primary image or story – the one he is pressured to lock on to - is one that tends to overshadow all other possibilities. And for most men, these are not roles that are discarded once grown and on their own in life. In my experience with men, time and time again, I have seen them carry that imagery into new families. Heroes become champions of their homes, often accomplishing great things, even as the wants and desires from their childhood become cold in the ground.

Lost children, who can become lost men, sometimes continue their needless lives in the service of others. They leave one family of which they demanded nothing and create another in which they do the same thing. They often, simply for lack of vision, pick women who need much and give little, just as their family of origin was willing to do.

Scapegoats, like heroes and lost children, tend to follow their life imagery to the same end. They pick women who will burden them with blame; women who will, just as their family did, refuse to look at their role in problems. Scapegoated men often have their choice of a lot of women. And there is no shortage of them who wind up alienated and carrying blame that does not belong to them.

The point here is not to say that men's lives are fixed in whatever was handed to them by their family. Quite the contrary. It would do most men well to remember that these are, on some level, luxurious problems. Humanity made it quite far without obsessive exploration of purpose and identity that are now modern indulgences.

Still, the accomplishments of men throughout ages made it possible to strain against the weight of a crisis in identity. We can now look at where we came from and maybe ponder a good bit longer on the story behind the story, the picture behind the picture that has always remained hidden. And we can perhaps decide more consciously what we want to be, and just as importantly, know why we are doing it.

The trick is in the ability to see that our lives are all in some sense a fiction, a story that we can still shape. It requires will. It requires a healthy sense of detachment, and by detachment, I mean the ability to stand back from your own story, from the pleasure and the pain and from any emotional investment in its outcome – at the puppeteer's distance. And it requires a creative mind.

Hillman said, and I am paraphrasing here, "rather than psychology, we undergo our best transformation when we engage in a craft – with our hands, intellectually, imaginatively or whatever. It can be knitting blankets, building boats, or constructing a philosophy…and as we come across difficult parts in those processes, in the craft, we untangle our own knots."

What I am suggesting here is that the transformation Hillman is referring to is the recrafting of our own story. That means to some degree throwing science and psychology out of the window. In the realm of human experience, science and psychology are equally useless.

It is the artist in you that matters. The writer. The creator. The builder of anything.

I wanted to write from a very early age. It was severely frowned upon by my parents. No, it was ridiculed. Not in overt terms, but in a quiet, nearly unspoken "be more like your hero brother" way. There is no real blame for that on them. They were simply people following the unconscious imagery we all lived by as a family. Still, the message set in and I did not write. Not for years and years.

Now I have written some 700+ essays and co-written three books. You are now reading my first completed set of works. I am not saying I have slain all my demons or finished the rewriting of my life story. I am just saying it is possible. And if a mug like me can do it, anyone can.

Made in the USA
Las Vegas, NV
11 July 2021